A Wee Bit Of Heaven

Cultivating A Lifestyle For Good Health And Survival

By
Frank Lichorobiec

**To order additional copies of this book,
go to www.creatspace.com/3698016**

Dedication

I dedicate this book to my wife, Roberta, and our five children, Marie, Karen, Frank, Jeffrey, and John

I wish to offer my heartfelt thanks
to my daughter Karen and Stephanie Moore
for the hours they spent in editing this book.

Preface

Long before the threat of a world financial meltdown, my wife, Roberta, my oldest daughter, Marie, and I have always felt that getting back to nature as a way of living is the only way to stay healthy and live longer. With my wife and I in our retirement years and starting to get our health in better order, we can now take an active part in a venture of taking control of what we eat and how we will live.

Five years ago, while living in Missouri, my eldest daughter, Marie and her family tried to do some small time farming by raising chickens and milk goats. She didn't have time to grow a garden, because she and her husband, at the time, had to go to work everyday. The chickens and goats were more than they could handle and still hold down a fulltime job. The relationship between Marie and her husband eventually broke up and the farming idea did also. This left Marie as a single mother who had to provide for herself, and the farm was now gone. The knowledge and experience didn't go away but the ability to continue in her venture for a better way of life, and healthy lifestyle did.

After their breakup, Roberta and I moved to Texas where we have been living for over three years. For the past two years, I have been fighting a chronic bone infection that could have cost me my foot due to diabetes. As God would have it, He led me to a great orthopedic surgeon who has been able to remove all the MRSA staff infection from the bone marrow of the infected bones, and I can now walk again without the aid of devices.

Marie's dream of a homestead lifestyle has never diminished; hopes linger that it will become a reality again. Roberta and I are planning on moving back to Missouri and living on a small farm close to where Marie is currently living. We hope this will help Marie with her dreams and will give us a place to finish out our golden years.

The advice that is found in "A Wee Bit Of Heaven" will be the same principles we will be putting into practice for our own lifestyle and survival. You know the old saying, "Practice what you preach," well that's exactly what we will be doing.

Contents

11.　Introduction

15.　Chapter 1- Why this book?
- Too many government controls
- We've become a nation of takers
- Impending world collapse
- A need for personal confidence when the going gets tough
- Don't wait for "*it*" to hit the fan; start now

27.　Chapter 2- Can we survive off the grid?
- A natural catastrophe can happen anywhere
- Emergency supply of medicine
- Emergency first aid supplies
- Learn basic first aid treatments
- What are the symptoms of a stroke?
- What should a bystander do?
- Emergency water and food supplies

- Dehydrated vs. freeze-dried food
- Take care of yourself first so you can later help your neighbors

43.   Chapter 3- Can we survive without doctors and medicine?

- The government is trying to regulate **Over The Counter** vitamins and drugs
- Drug companies want to control all OTCs
- Common sense approach to health care
- Healing herbs in the Holy Bible
- Get rid of the TV and read more

61.   Chapter 4- Can we survive without supermarkets?

- Consider homesteading
- Getting started
- Livestock, vegetables, and fruit trees
- Look at all the health benefits
- Storing and processing what you produce
- Canning fresh fruits and vegetables

109. Chapter 5- City and Suburban Self Reliance

- Time to be creative
- Raising chickens inside city limits
- Raising rabbits inside city limits
- Raising miniature goats
- Small fruit trees

151.   Chapter 6- Can we survive alone or do we need others?

- A community of like believers
- Strength in numbers
- Looking out for one another
- Using the barter system

165.   Chapter 7- Where does God or religion fit into this picture?

- Design by Robert Frost
- NOW YOU SEE IT AND NOW YOU DON'T
- Mind, body, and spirit
- What is spiritual healing?
- Age of enlightenment

193.   Chapter 8- We are living longer than our ancestors

- What is driving us as we look towards the future?

- Looking at the big picture
- Do hard times determine your future?

203. **Conclusion**

205. **Index**

Introduction

After writing my first three books, which are spiritual in nature, I have decided to change course a little for this next one. I felt inspired to write on a different subject; I feel the world and my family must be prepared for.

As in my previous books, I am writing about my latest inspiration and lifestyle changes I am going through in my life. Many of these lifestyle changes are brought about by both external and internal conditions, events, and changes in my life. Conditions such as health, both good and bad, survival for both my wife and I as we face our golden years, and what to do when world conditions get worse and not better.

Almost every chapter in this book can and may be published as a stand-alone book but why go out and buy dozens of books when I can put a lot of helpful ideas in each chapter?

This past June of 2011, I turned 70 and believe me when I say, I have studied and experienced a lot in life. I find when I am in conversation with people and some subject matter comes up that they don't quite understand, something about it, I usually have either experienced it, or read about it, or studied the subject matter.

If you read my first book titled, "Truth Will Set You Free" A Spiritual Awakening Of A Retired Minister, you would see my spiritual autobiography that has taken me through many different walks of life and experiences. So for those who haven't read it, I will summarize some of what I have done or accomplished in life.

I was the second child born of Polish parents, born in 1941, raised Catholic, in a poor household. Being both poor and Polish helped to form a very close-knit family bond. Though I was born after the depression, I knew that my parents had to go without many things taken for granted today, because of World War II.

I remember how my mother learned to stretch the family food budget and raise some of our food from the garden in the back yard. Back then many families had fruit trees and gardens, from which they shared much of their bounty with each other.

After high school, I went to community College to become an electro mechanical drafting designer. With that knowledge, I worked at General Electric in the Heavy Military Division on Government Projects, such as the Atlas Missile. Later, I studied and got my insurance license to sell life insurance in New York State where I was living at the time. I also sold new and used cars at a Ford Dealership before getting hired as a full time fireman in the City of Fulton, NY. Seven years later, I felt the need to go off to college to become a preacher in the Christian Faith.

After graduating from Dallas Christian College with a bachelor's degree in Pastoral Ministries, I worked either full-time or part-time for many congregations around the country for over thirty years. I took an interest in studying many religious organizations and philosophies. I studied spiritual healing, holistic health treatments, dietary health foods for healing and the practice of positive thinking. I have run my own business both before, and after my full time preaching ended. My ministries have taken me from the North East to the South West, to the West Coast, the North West, and Mid West. I have seen and ministered to the rich and the poor, mostly the not so well off lower to middle class. I have seen suffering, sickness, and down and out homeless people trying to survive in this wonderful county of ours.

I share this information with you to show that after 70 years of age, I feel I am somewhat qualified to write on this subject matter. I believe we are being poisoned daily with much of the food we buy at the super markets, whether processed in cans or injected with growth hormones and fertilized with all types of chemicals and pesticides. I will cover how and what we can do to save our health from these things and do so wherever you may want to live; whether in the country, suburbs, or in an apartment complex. Being a farmer with lots of land isn't the only way to grow your own poison-free food, but it does help.

With our future held in balance and not knowing if the American dollar will be worth anything, I have some ideas on how we may cope with this situation if it shall occur. The future of our spiritual way of thinking about The Creator Of All Things (God) will also be discussed. "A Wee Bit Of Heaven" is not the answer to all things, but will get you started on the road to self-reliance and good health.

Frank Lichorobiec

Cedar Park, Texas

Chapter One

Why this book?

Too many government controls

Where has our freedom gone? Are we raising a nation of imbeciles that belong locked and protected so they can't hurt themselves? The government must think that is what we are. Over the 70 years of my life, I have seen this country's freedom disappear through big-government regulations and control. Big government seems to think that we can't think for ourselves. They are either outlawing something or taxing it to the point where the public can't afford to buy it. And that is the point of the tax. The government gains tax money and at the same time controls the masses by saying they know what's good or bad for us.

Every time a new tax or some kind of control is implemented, for whatever reason, it often becomes unpopular with the masses. Now, does this sound like a government for the people and by the people to you?   It doesn't to me. When I was about 12 years old, I bought my first 22-caliber rifle. At this early age, I learned to hunt and became a very responsible person in the use of firearms. By the time I was 16, I received my first shotgun where I could go rabbit, pheasant, duck and deer hunting. It was a time when we could walk down the streets of our small hometowns carrying our shotguns and a large hunting knife strapped to our hips. No one was concerned and call the police out of fear. Think about it: when was the last time you saw a gun rack in the back window of a pickup?

Big government, and that include state and local governments, has taken or restricted most of our rights we enjoyed 50 years ago. Don't they know that there is a basic tendency that if you take something away from someone, they tend to want it even more and to the point where they will get it even if it's illegal? Look what happened during the prohibition against alcohol. Now if you say that the public can have something, like cigarettes, then most people may not want it after they become aware of its health hazards. However, take it away and see what will happen.

As I write this book rumors are going around that some states, in order to stop the growing spread of obesity, want to charge a $1.00 tax on every donut sold. Now how ridiculous is that? If I want a donut, and I had to pay the price of a donut plus a one-dollar government imposed tax, I would make my own, until it becomes illegal to possess sugar. It's getting a little ridiculous lately but as long as the government financially supports a great majority of the population, then government feels they have the right to do as they please.

We've become a nation of takers

Stephen Moore, senior economics writer for The Wall Street Journal editorial page, wrote, "If you want to understand better why so many states—from New York to Wisconsin to California—are teetering on the brink of bankruptcy, consider this depressing statistic: Today in America there are nearly twice as many people working for the government (22.5 million) than in all of manufacturing (11.5 million). This is an almost exact reversal of the situation in 1960, when there were 15 million workers in manufacturing and 8.7 million collecting a paycheck from the government."

'It gets worse. More Americans work for the government than work in construction, farming, fishing, forestry, manufacturing, mining and utilities combined. We have moved decisively from a nation of makers to a nation of takers. Nearly half of the $2.2 trillion cost of

state and local governments is the $1 trillion-a-year tab for pay and benefits of state and local employees. Is it any wonder that so many states and cities cannot pay their bills?"
(Wall Street Journal, April 1, 2011, Opinion Page by Stephen Moore, "We've Become A Nation Of Takers, Not Makers")

I would like for you to think about what you have just read. What happens when the Government can't pay its own bills? What happens to all those people or at least most of them? They go on to the welfare roles that millions of Americans are currently on and if the government can't pay their bills, what makes you think they will pay welfare? .

"From exertion come wisdom and purity; from sloth ignorance and sensuality" – Thoreau

These words aptly describe the welfare state and the havoc government entitlement programs and concessions that big labor coerces from the public and private sector wreak upon the American landscape and the free-enterprise system under the masquerade of social justice. Social justice encourages Americans and even illegal aliens to become wards of the State. And what happens when you become a ward of the State? You became a sloth that becomes, as well as breeds, ignorance and sensuality. This dependency usually leads to generations of dependency on the Government. We have become a Nation of takers and not makers.

It's just a matter of time when Big Brother can no longer keep taxing the wealthy to feed the poor who don't work. I'm not saying that everyone on social welfare is a sloth, but the incentive is not there to do better for yourself. That day is approaching, very soon, when the Government may collapse. That may be sooner than you think..

Impending world collapse

There is an impending world collapse, and it is at hand in the USA. It seems most people won't figure it out until it is too late. The USA is on the brink of total economic collapse. The Euro is replacing the Dollar and the world's reserve currency as the dollar sinks to record lows every day. Still, this is only the beginning of what will be the chaotic downfall of the United States.

The demise of the United States as the global superpower could come far more quickly than anyone imagines. If Washington is dreaming of 2040 or 2050 as the end of the American Century, a more realistic assessment of domestic and global trends suggests that in 2025, just 14 years henceforth, it could all be over except for the shouting.

A look at what's happening, this year in 2011, with many foreign governments in chaos or collapse, we need to look at what most empires project. We need to look at their history, and it should remind us that they are fragile organisms. So delicate is their ecology of power that, when things start to go truly bad, empires regularly unravel with unholy speed. Just a year for Portugal, two years for the Soviet Union, eight years for France, 11 years for the Ottomans, 17 years for Great Britain, and, in all likelihood, 22 years for the United States, counting from the crucial year 2003.

The-head-of-the-worlds-biggest-hedge-fund-sees-economic-collapse-due-to-money-print-ing-by-early-2013. The article, which was originally published on a blog called Zero Hedge, tells how Ray Dalio — head of Bridgewater, the world's biggest hedge fund — predicts the collapse of the economy in "late 2012 or early 2013? due to money printing. He says that countries heavily in debt, including the US, will print more money to deal with it. "There hasn't been a case in history where they haven't eventually printed money and devalued their currency," he said in an interview printed in *The New Yorker.*

A need for personal confidence when the going gets tough

Has the reality set in yet? Should we all drink the poisoned Kool-Aid because we see no hope for the future? This is why I chose to write this book. I have written things that can offset what may become a struggle for existence. Many of these things, if taken to heart, should help to give you some personal confidence to survive the hard times that may be coming.

Young or old, we all need to be prepared for what may come your way. Let's say the economy doesn't collapse and the Government finds someway to pull itself out of the quagmire it has gotten itself into. There are other reasons to be prepared. In the last two years, the world has suffered some of the most devastating disasters that it has ever seen.

The earthquakes in Japan nearly wiped out half their nation. There were tsunamis so large they flattened major cities around the world. Many tornados across the Mid West have leveled entire cities and caused countless dollars of damage. The hottest heat wave this nation has seen in many years has taken many lives and caused many people to live without electricity for hours and even days. The heat wave has also cause one of the largest wild fires that Arizona ever had.

Due to climate change, we may no longer be

able to count on familiar patterns of rain and snow and river flow to refill our urban reservoirs, irrigate our farms and power our dams. While farmers in the Midwest were recovering from the spring flood of 2008 (in some areas, the second "100-year flood" in 15 years). Farmers in California and Texas allowed crop lands to lie fallow and sent cattle to early slaughter to cope with the drought of 2009.

During the continuing dry conditions in 2011, Texas forecasters said the devastating drought, which has led to brown lawns and empty swimming pools in the cities and has caused more than $5 billion in damages to the state's farmers and ranchers could continue for another nine years.

So it isn't just an economical disaster we need to worry about, but natural disasters that may come our way. Will you be ready when it happens? Or are you going to panic and throw in the towel and give up.

Being prepared is a Boy Scout motto. I was a Boy Scout when I was growing up, and I have always felt a sense of confidence that I am prepared when something comes my way. And when you acquire the personal confidence you need, you will tend to remain calm in all situations while asking yourself what needs to be done to get out of this current situation. It's all

about preparedness and knowing how to survive when the going gets tough.

Don't wait for "*it*" to hit the fan; start now

Here are some of the attitudes many in this
country may take; denial where one will say
that all this is hogwash and do nothing; pro-
crastination where one will say yes I believe
things could and may happen but then will do
nothing and just wait; and lastly, you will find
those who believe and trust only in God, and
do nothing.

First of all, I believe and know we must trust in
God. He lives in me, and I am his creation that
He loves very deeply. However, the scriptures
say, that faith without works is dead. Let me
tell you a story. There was this little old lady
who lived in a small country house all by herself. Her house was in a 100-year flood plane.
Well, one day it started raining really hard and
all the up-land streams and waterways started
to swell to their max. All indications showed
that the floodwaters were on their way to over-
take this little farmhouse. The sheriff's dept
was sent to worn all the people in the path of
the impending flood. So when the sheriff came
to this little old lady's house and told her to
pack up and move out, all she would say is I
trust in God and am going to stay. The sheriff

could do nothing but leave her there.

Well, the floodwaters came and started to rise all around her house. She was forced to go to her second floor to stay safe. This time the Sheriff came by with his boat and told this little old lady to get in before she drowns. All she would say is that she trusts in God and is not leaving. All the sheriff could do was just leave here there. As the floodwaters rose to the point where she could no longer stay on the second floor, she was forced to go up on the roof to keep safe. This time the Sheriff came by with a helicopter and told her that this is her last chance to save herself. Again, all she would say is, "I trust in God, and He will save me." After the sheriff left without her the floodwater finally came and overtook her house, and she died in the flood.

When she got to heaven and stood before God, she said, God why didn't you save me from drowning." God's response was this, "I sent you a sheriff's car to take you away, and you wouldn't get in. I then sent you a boat, and you still wouldn't get in. Finally I sent you a helicopter and still you did nothing. I sent you all this help and you turned me down." So you see God is always with us and He sometimes leaves the miracles we expect to be done by his servants here on Earth. Jesus said, "Whatever you have done for the least of my brothers, you have done for me." (Mathew 25:40)

So don't wait for *"it"* to hit the fan; start now. Life may not seem like you need to do anything at this time, but it's later than you think. By the way, if you ever worked in a dairy barn with all those cows in their milking stalls, you will know what that *"it"* is.

Chapter 2

Can we survive off the grid?

Western Society is in confusion; the industrial world is teetering on a collapse, and it looks like things could get worse. With a society of takers and reliance on our Government to keep everything going, it is quite possible that many people who have relied on a failing system for their means of survival will very soon find that they have made a mistake of historic proportions. Historical, because every major "classical" culture went down the same road our society is on today.

A natural catastrophe can happen anywhere

I don't want to sound like doom and gloom, so let's leave the demise of Western Society for a moment and look at natural catastrophes. I lived in Upstate New York, in the small city of Fulton. My wife Roberta gave birth to our first child,

Marie, in September of 1966. In the early part of December that same year while visiting my parents out in the country, we became snowed in and couldn't get out for two solid weeks.

Now here we were with a couple of bottles of formula and just a hand full of diapers, (we didn't use disposables then), and maybe one or two changes of baby clothes, not to mention my wife and I didn't have a change of clothes either.

The snowdrifts were packed very hard and piled so high that no plow could begin to open any of the local roads. The fire department in the city couldn't make it up any side streets and had to drag hose lines to fight fires a block or more from where they could get. It was a major disaster that cut hundreds, if not thousands, off from needed food supplies and basic essentials.

Besides all the obvious things needed, think what you would do when your toilet paper runs out, and you are snowed in for two or more weeks. It's not a pretty picture, is it? Well, this is what my father, mother, my wife, our new young baby, and I were facing. Thank God our nearest neighbor was close enough for me to make it to his place walking in waist-deep snow to see if he could help us. He happened to have a couple of sets of snowshoes, so we put them on and walked over 2 miles to the city limits where there was a small super market. Needless to say, I was able to buy much of the essentials we needed to survive this natural disaster.

Now you might say, that what happened in New York could have been expected, and everyone should be prepared. And you are right. Even so, how about being snowed in on a mountain in California. Well, 38 years later while preaching in a mountain community in California called Frazier Park, we had a similar situation. The snow came harder and longer than usual. The heavy snow took down a lot of power lines and even transmission towers. The entire mountain was without electricity, including the home the church provided for us. One of God's blessing was the house we lived in was heated with gas, and we had walled heaters that would work without electricity. It didn't blow the heat around the house like when the fans were working, but if we sat near the heaters, we could feel warm.

Our kitchen stove was a gas stove, so we were able to cook food. We had a wood-burning stove in the living/dining room, and plenty of wood piled outside. We had plenty of candles, even though they were the scented kind in the large jars, but we managed to see when the sun went down. Our electricity came back on two weeks later and we realized what changes we must make in the future in order to survive off the grid.

Emergency supply of medicine

If you find yourself snowed in or in the middle of any other disaster, you may not think much about medical supplies. However, I believe medical supplies are more important than food. Let me explain what happened to me not too long ago. I am a type 1 diabetic on an insulin pump. Usually there is about a 2 to 3 day supply of insulin in the pump.

One weekend my wife and I decided to take a trip to see our daughter Karen and grandchildren that lived three and one-half hours away. With the price of gas that it is, we only travel to see them about four times a year and stay for 3 to five days at a time. We arrived Saturday around noon and were planning on staying until Tuesday morning. Well, Saturday night, while getting ready for bed, I noticed that my pump was getting low and figured I had enough insulin in the pump to last until morning. When morning came, and I was getting my supplies out of my carrying case, I was shocked to find out that I had forgotten to pack my bottles of insulin.

You guessed it. Right after breakfast, we

packed up and headed back home on an empty pump. We decided not to go back after traveling home with another three and one-half hour trip.

Because of this situation, I began to think, what would I do if my pharmacy ran out of my type of insulin, and I didn't have any way of getting any for some period of time? I use about five bottles of insulin a month and was only ordering about a month's supply to keep on hand. Now I take advantage of the 90-day supply program and feel somewhat safe if some natural disaster happens, and I can't get out to get my insulin. This also holds true for all the medications that you are taking.

Another thing you may do, ask your doctor if you need to take the full dosage everyday? Some medications has a 24 to 48 hours residual effect, and if you should miss a dosage and it's close to another dosage time, they tell you to skip the missed dosage and get back on schedule. Now I emphasize, with the doctor's approval, ask him if you were to take a full dose one day and maybe a half dose another day, would it be harmful to your health? Some medications are critical and some may not be so critical, if you are taking them for prevention only. If you get the doctor's ok, take one half dosage every other day, then every 30 days, you can save as much as 7 ½ pills of whatever you are taking, left over.

Now be aware of when you would normally run out and then renew your prescription as usual. Do this every month and in four months you will have an extra 30-day supply. At the end of a year you will have a 90-day supply, etc. This will help when you can't get out and get your medications refilled. One word of caution, keep rotating them so they don't overrun the expiration date listed on the bottle.

Emergency first aid supplies

If I were to ask you to go through your first-aid kit (if you even have one) and see if it is up to date with the supplies it came with when you first bought it or put it together, what would you find? Most don't even have anything more than a glove box size for your car and a box or two of Band-Aids in your medicine cabinet. Before I would try to tell you what you need in an emergency first-aid kit, to be used in times of disaster, I suggest you go to a medical supply store or your local pharmacy and speak to a professional for advice. There are a lot of things we never think about when it comes to first aid. For example, Dermal Wound Cleanser is a first aid antiseptic for cleaning wounds. Don't count on fresh clean water in a disaster, as there may not be any for wound cleansing. Something else that doesn't come in first-aid kits is a splint to hold broken bones together until professional help arrives. Then there are the blankets and sheets you need to set aside in plastic bags, specifically for first aid use.

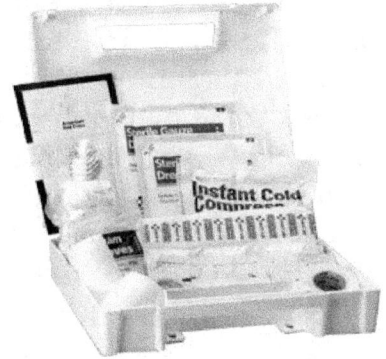

Typical Bulk First Aid Kit (25 person, ANSI complaint)

Are you beginning to get the picture where most of us fall short on our ability to handle an emergency? Don't think I am trying to replace our emergency rooms at the hospital, but it may be hours and in some cases days before help arrives.

Learn basic first aid treatments

What good is having your entire first aid supplies ready if you don't know what to do in case of an emergency? Learning first aid can be done by taking first aid courses offered in your local communities. It is just important to know CPR because the first few moments of a heart attack are very important to saving lives. Check with your local health clinics or fire department and see if and when they may offer this course to the public. CPR techniques have recently changed where all you now do is just keep pumping the patient below their sternum until help arrives. No more need to stop and breath air into their lungs. Anyone can learn this technique very easily and be able to save a life.

It helps to know the telltale signs of heart attacks, chocking, and a stroke. The first two, you will learn when you take first aid courses. The stroke is one that you don't need to take a course for, but you need to know when it happens so that you can get professional help. The earlier a stroke victim gets medical aid, the better chance for full recovery. Because stroke injures the brain, you may not realize that you are having a stroke i it happens to you. To a bystander, someone having a stroke may just look unaware or confused. Stroke victims have the best chance if someone around them recognizes the symptoms and acts quickly.

What are the symptoms of a stroke?

The symptoms of stroke are distinct because they happen quickly:
1. Sudden numbness or weakness of the face, arm, or leg (especially on one side of the body)
2. Sudden confusion, trouble speaking or understanding speech
3. Sudden trouble seeing in one or both eyes
4. Sudden trouble walking, dizziness, loss of balance or coordination
5. Sudden severe headache with no known cause

What should a bystander do?

If you believe someone is having a stroke – if he or she suddenly loses the ability to speak, or move an arm or leg on one side, or experience facial paralysis on one side – call 911 immediately. And if any of these systems hit you, don't wait for them to subside, get help right away. Stroke is a medical emergency. Every minute counts when someone is having a stroke. The longer blood flow is cut off to the brain, the greater the damage. Immediate treatment can save people's lives and enhance their chances for successful recovery.

Emergency water and food supplies

Whether you live in a region prone to natural disasters, or if you are emergency survival preparedness minded, it is imperative that you store water for you and your family, before you think about storing food.

A human cannot survive without water for more than just a few days in a hot environment or at most maybe a week in a colder environment. That may seem unreal to some, but it is true.

The human body is about 60 to 75 percent water by weight. We normally get our water, H2O, from not only the beverages that we drink but also from the foods that we eat. We can live much longer without food. Most doctors agree 4 to 6 weeks maximum. This is why it is so important to build a water storage supply first, before you think about food storage.

Here is a very simple, economic, and practical way to build up survival storage of safe drinking water. First, obtain as many "food grade" five-gallon buckets that fit the following formula: One gallon of water per person per day. This means survival water for one person for one-month equals 30 gallons, or six five-gallon buckets.

To be safe, the buckets should be food grade. You can find deals on quantity purchases of Food grade five-gallon buckets, which are usually white (not always), and will have an icon on the bottom of the bucket that reads HDPE #2. HDPE #2 buckets that are not food grade will have been manufactured with a non-food-grade "mold release agent" and leach into the container, and whatever is in the container.

These five-gallon buckets of water should be dumped and refilled with fresh filtered water every six months. If you don't have a water filter, it may be a good idea to get one and not have to pay the price for store bought bottled water.

The next important aspect of survival during a natural catastrophe is your food supply when you can't get to a market and stock up after disaster strikes. Have you ever seen the run on a super market when there are hurricane warnings? The shelves empty very fast. To avoid this, have basic emergency food storage in your home that will last a long time without refrigeration.

The best place to get the long-lasting, just add water and eat type of food can be found in outfitter stores. Many will have a whole section on survival foods and equipment to prepare you, if needed. I'm not saying you can't find survival food, such as freeze dried or can food, at your local supermarket, but they usually handle food for day-to-day use but you need to think long term.

Canned food is usually ideal for survival situations if you are stuck in a home. However canned goods will stay edible depending on the type of container and food stored in it. If your cans are stored properly, they can last up to two years. Examples include canned meats, fish and peanut butter.

Freeze-dried or dehydrated foods are the ultimate survival food source. They are easy to store, light and can stay fresh for 30 years. A six-week supply of food can fit under your bed. Furthermore, contrary to the sound of it, many dehydrated foods are quite tasty. If you decide to purchase freeze-dried or dehydrated foods, you can choose anything from lasagna to beef stew. Just add water, and you have a meal.

Dehydrated vs. freeze-dried food

A lot of people are unsure about the differences between dehydrated foods and freeze dried foods. Both foods are optimum for long term storage, offering essentially the same shelf life for the same type of products. The real difference is found in these areas:

Taste

Dehydrated foods are without any seasoning or additional ingredients (usually). There are some exceptions to this, found in the "mixes" and the soups and stews available. Some products do contain multiple ingredients and can be used to make a complete meal without adding anything.

But many of the other products are single ingredients. For example, rice. It's just rice, the same rice that you can buy in the supermarket. Survival type products are all packaged for long-term storage in cans, buckets or even pouches, which makes a decided difference in terms of freshness, nutrition and shelf life. There are also a number of products packaged in bags. Bagged products should be put in airtight containers for long-term storage, or simply used.

Dehydrated foods require cooking and seasoning. Cooking times vary, but most are added to boiling water. You can also do "thermos cooking" by adding boiling water to a thermos, adding ingredients and letting it sit for a couple of hours. Just forget about it, it will cook itself. This will cook the food slowly using the minimum amount of energy.

Freeze dried foods, on the other hand, are usually foods containing a multitude of ingredients and seasonings. Nothing more is needed.

A little cook time in hot water to re-hydrate and have them ready just to eat. They are pre-seasoned, pre-cooked and pre-mixed with other ingredients, making them the fastest, easiest and tastiest foods available.

Seasoning
Keep on hand your favorite seasonings. Dehydrated food should be seasoned for best taste. The freeze-dried entrees won't need any at all, unless you're one of those that drowns everything in ketchup. You can even make ketchup from tomato powder....

Ingredients
Freeze dried food is usually an "entree", containing multiple items for a complete meal. Most dishes have several items included within them and you don't need to do any other cooking or adding ingredients to make a complete meal. Because it's freeze dried, you simply add hot water, or add the product to hot water and cook for about 10 minutes. These re-hydrate the food completely and it's ready to eat!

Dehydrated foods are usually single ingredients. You can mix any dehydrated food with any other food product for a combination of tastes, textures and varieties.

Take care of yourself first so you can later help your neighbors

Have you ever been on a plane and before take-off, the flight attendant goes over the instructions in case of an emergency? They say your oxygen masks will drop down from a above compartment and you are to pull it straight down on your mask to get the oxygen flowing. Then place it over your nose and mouth before you help a child or elderly person who is having problems. The reason for that is to be able to maintain your own oxygen levels in order to help others.

This same principle holds true in case of emergencies. If you are badly cut and bleeding, and you don't do something to stop your bleeding, you may pass out before you can be of any help to others. Your first priority is yourself, your family and then your neighbors. It may sound selfish to think of yourself before you think of your neighbors, but look what the apostle Paul told Timothy in his first letter. 1st Timothy 5:8 (KJV) "But if any provide not for his own, and specially for those of his own house, he hath denied the faith, and is worse than an infidel." I know this verse is stretching it a little, but I think you can get the point.

Chapter 3

Can we survive without doctors and medicine?

The question posed in this chapter's title is an important one. The answer to the question is: we may have to some time soon. If the government gets its way, everything that we can use naturally to improve our health will be considered a drug and under their control. We may have to learn the ways of the medicine doctors of ancient times. We may need to grow our own healing health foods and medicines. It's a scary outlook into the future but one never knows. First come government controls, and then an economic meltdown leaving life very uncertain.

From NEW YORK (Reuters) Friday August 5, 2011 – "The United States lost its top-notch AAA credit rating from Standard & Poor's on Friday in an unprecedented reversal of fortune for the world's largest economy." When the government loses its credit rating, it loses its borrowering power. Right now our government is running on borrowed money and is running out of time. Once it runs out of money to pay its bills, doctors and hospitals will not get their money for services rendered and then comes a medical meltdown. But in the mean time, the government is acting like nothing is wrong and still trying to control all aspects of our medical wellness.

The government is trying to regulate Over The Counter vitamins and drugs

Big Government just never stops. Senator Durbin recently (before the start of this book, during the Summer of 2011) introduced the Dietary Supplement Labeling Act. This bill requires that the FDA, together with the Institute of Medicine, compile a list of dietary ingredients that could lead to adverse events or are otherwise deemed risky in some way — based on completely arbitrary or non-existent standards. Once an ingredient or supplement is on the list, there is no clear process to challenge the FDA and IOM determination, not even if new or contradictory evidence comes to light. DSHEA, the Nutrition Labeling and Education Act, GMP standards, and the Fair Packaging and Labeling Act all ensure the safety of nutritional supplements and provide guidelines for clear and comprehensive labeling.

This bill uses vague language to create extraneous red tape, paperwork, and burdensome labeling requirements, when everything the bill mandates other than its new and arbitrary disapproval process is already being accomplished under current law! Congressional intent turns it into a pre-approval process with unknown and therefore completely arbitrary standards. The Dietary Supplement Labeling Act and the new FDA NDI guidance both comes out of the same script book: they both essentially give government agencies the right to say no to new supplements on completely arbitrary grounds. And the new FDA NDI guidance also tries to turn any supplement into a "new" supplement and thus subject to the desired pre-approval process. What is needed is enforcement, not new legislation. This bill may also have far-reaching consequences. For example, if the FDA and IOM draw up their arbitrary list of "safe" supplements and amounts — such as no vitamin D in amounts greater than 4000 IU — as provided for in this bill, more therapeutic supplement doses or preparations would never meet the new hurdle set by the FDA's new guidance on New Dietary Ingredients.

I am greatly concerned about the FDA's draft guidance on New Dietary Ingredient notifications for dietary supplements. It turns what was meant to be a simple notification system into a scheme where the FDA can approve — or deny — any supplement created in the past seventeen years, making the FDA the ultimate arbiter of what dietary supplements will and will not be available. The FDA has already refused to "file" (turns down) most notifications of new supplements. If the new guidance is accepted, new supplements will be a rarity. It is all completely arbitrary. The agency's interpretation of "new dietary ingredient" is far too broad. Under the new rules, all ingredients in the food supply before 1994 that have been chemically altered in any way are considered NDIs and therefore subject to NDI notification. Moreover, the definition of "chemically altered" includes certain types of fermentation and exposure of ingredients to high-temperature baking and cooking, and using a botanical ingredient at a different life stage than previously used — for example, an extract of unripened apples instead of ripe apples. How absurd! The guidance states that a synthetic copy of a constituent or extracts of an herb or other botanical is not considered a dietary ingredient. This arbitrary distinction will make many dietary ingredients on the market illegal — particularly as this standard does not apply to non-botanicals.

Most importantly, the guidance makes the NDI notification process burdensome and repetitive. It requires a different notification for the same ingredient for every different version of the supplement it is in — for example, the same ingredient at a higher concentration needs a separate notification/approval. Yet, the same ingredient in a different combination of ingredients requires another notification/approval. The Dietary Supplement Health and Education Act of 1994 states that "the Federal Government should not take any actions to impose unreasonable regulatory barriers limiting or slowing the flow of safe products and accurate information to consumers." It says that Congress finds that "dietary supplements are safe within a broad range of intake, and safety problems with the supplements are relatively rare." And it says "legislative action that protects the right of access of consumers to safe dietary supplements is necessary in order to promote wellness."

The guidance may also have far-reaching consequences. For example, if Sen. Durbin's dangerous Dietary Supplement Labeling Act goes forward, with the list of "safe" supplements and doses which FDA and IOM would draw up under the bill — such as vitamin D in amounts greater than 4000 IU — it would mean that more therapeutic doses or supplement preparations could never meet the new NDI hurdle. This could have a profoundly negative impact on this nation's health. This draft guidance does the exact opposite of what Congress intended. It imposes unreasonable barriers that limit and slow the flow of safe products and accurate information to consumers.

Drug companies want to control all OTCs

If the government gets its way, they will allow the drug companies to dispense all OTC dietary supplements and low-grade medicines such as those used for the common cold.

Recent studies have emerged showing that some elements in lemons can help to alleviate the effects of cancer and the side effects of medical treatment for cancer. They can also help in the prevention of cancer and possibly, the movement or growth of cancer cells.

Whether it is taken in the form of lemon juice, as a lemon essential oil or as the lemon itself to flavor another type of food or drink, one can access the cancer prevention and treatment qualities of the wonderful fruit that is lemon.

Now why did I make this statement? A Reference Manual entitled "Biological Theory of Ionization" by Dr. Carey A. Reams where Reams said, "lemon juice is the only anionic substance, the only natural hydrochloric acid on earth, that I know of."

He further went on to explain: "it's anionic, electrons travel clockwise, all food we eat are cationic with the exception of lemon and if there is another I never found it, when it goes into the system it can be converted into some 6 billion different enzymes with less chemical change than any other natural substance known to man."

Lemon juice taken with water he claimed— "taken periodically helps the liver. It takes 18 hours to form an amino acid in your body. That's one of the reasons you need that small little shot of lemon juice, for your liver, spread throughout the day. Lemon juice is nothing more than dilute hydrochloric acid."

In a recent report from the Institute of Health Sciences, 819 N. L.L.C. Cause Street, Baltimore, MD, lemon (Citrus) is a miraculous product that kills cancer cells. It is 10,000 times stronger than chemotherapy.

Why do we not know about that? Because there are laboratories interested in making a synthetic version that will bring them huge profits. The source of this information is fascinating as it comes from one of the largest drug manufacturers in the world. It states that after more than 20 laboratory tests since 1970, the lemon extracts revealed that it destroys the malignant cells in 12 cancers, including colon, breast, prostate, lung and pancreas. The compounds of this tree showed 10,000 times better than the product Adriamycin, a drug normally used chemotherapeutic in the world, slowing the growth of cancer cells. And what is even more astonishing: this type of therapy with lemon extracts only destroys malignant cancer cells and it does not affect healthy cells.

The sad part for the drug companies is they have not been able to make a synthetic pill to do what the lemon juice itself can do. And look at how long they have kept this secret from the public. It has become obvious that they don't have our best interest at heart; just how to make themselves rich.

Common sense approach to health care

Now don't be foolish and stop all your medications and go holistic in health care, (not just yet), as some advocates would have you do. I believe in holistic and homeopathic treatments for your health, and I would suggest you start taking this approach first and when you start to see the desired results, then tell your doctor you want to cut back on the strength of your medications.

If your desired results continue to improve, then repeat the above process of asking your doctor until you have weaned yourself off all medication. There may be some conditions you are treating, and that could cause you serious or fatal results if stopped. Do research and find out if others are treating the same condition holistically or homeopathically. You may be able to start using God's natural remedies and eventually wean off of them also.

However, in any case, caution is recommended when it comes to your health. If it's already too late, and you find yourself without the ability to use conventional drugs, then do what you have to in order to save your life. The natural holistic or homeopathic approach may be your only option.

Healing herbs in the Holy Bible

Holistic or homeopathic healing got its roots back during the creation of the Earth.

Gen. 1:29 (KJV) And God said, "Behold, I have given you every herb bearing seed, which is upon the face of all the earth, and every tree, in the which is the fruit of a tree yielding seed; to you it shall be for meat."

Ezekiel 47:12 "Fruit trees of all kinds will grow on both banks of the river. Their leaves will not wither, nor will their fruit fail. Every month they will bear fruit, because the water from the sanctuary flows to them. Their fruit will serve for food and their leaves for **healing**."

Modern doctors, scientists and researchers can scoff at herbs and herbal therapies all they like. However, when they do, who and what, really, are they laughing at? You? The herbs? Or the Creator Himself?

Before we begin, I want to remind you to use this material in the spirit with which it was written not as a be-all, end-all of books on medicinal herbs, but as a starting point from which to begin your own thorough investigation of the bounty to be harvested from God's Healing Garden.

Herbs, seeds and nuts, from the almond to walnut have many suggested healing properties by many herbalists. When it comes to survival, let me share some of what I feel are important ones that you can find most anywhere.

Almond

Almonds are a storehouse of vitamins and nutrients, including vitamin magnesium, magnesium and arginine, and dietary fiber, so much so that many herbalists believe that two or three almonds a day can protect you from most sickness. Considered brain food by many, almonds also are said to combat the agony of impotence as well. This is a delicious, inexpensive health insurance that's well worth considering in your life.

Aloe

The aloe mentioned so prominently in the Bible is not the typical aloe vera plant from which we derive the gels, juices and powders that are highly respected as medicinal herbs today. Many if not most folks aren't aware of the difference and assume that Biblical aloe, a tree for which there is no known medicinal use, is the same.

Aloe Vera is widely grown in the Holy Land today, and it is an extremely safe and effective treatment for scrapes, cuts, burns, bedsores and other skin problems. Taken internally as juice or in capsule form, aloe is soothing to the entire intestinal tract. Widespread testimony indicates it can ease the pain of arthritis and other inflammatory conditions. Aloe also is considered to be a powerful laxative for occasional use.

Apple

What can't you say about the apple as a weapon in your personal war against illnesses of all kinds? An apple a day, as the saying goes, keeps the doctor away - and it's no mystery why. Apples are chock full of vitamins - vitamin C especially - and one of the finest blood cleansers around.

Of particular importance, health-wise, is the presence of pectin, a substance that research has shown to block receptors on the surface of cancer calls, flush environmental toxins from the body, lower cholesterol, reduce the risk of heart disease and more. Strong research indicates that apples are a tremendous heart tonic, stabilize blood sugar levels, kill viruses, and suppress appetite, making them a first-rate diet food.

Beans

You might not think of beans as herbs but they most certainly are. Not only that, they're featured prominently in the Bible. When the authors of the Bible spoke of beans, they were referring to a wide variety - much like the selection we enjoy today. Beans, of course, are a sensational source of low- fat protein and more vitamins and minerals than you can shake a stick at.

Furthermore, beans are just the kind of healthful, high-fiber food, we all need plenty of to keep our cholesterol in check; and our colons working smoothly and regularly. Rich in carbohydrates as well as the important amino acids our bodies do not produce on their own and need from an outside source. If you are dieting, beans can and should be an indispensable menu item. Studies confirm that beans are appetite suppressants, taking the edge off hunger pangs for four hours or more after you eat them, eliminating the desire for snacks.

Corn

When the Bible mentions corn, say scholars, the authors were referring to wheat, barley and other crops, not corn as we think of it. For the record, sweet corn and its components have several solid medicinal uses.

Corn silk

This herb, which most folks throw away, eases urination complaints, is a diuretic and is often used by men with benign enlargement of the prostate. Corn itself lowers the risk of cancer and heart disease, and fights tooth decay.

Dill

A digestive aid of the first order, dill relieves intestinal gas (flatulence) as well. Studies suggest that dill can reduce blood pressure by dilating blood vessels, stimulating respiration and slowing the heart rate.

Figs

One of the oldest medicinal herbs known to man, figs are used in the treatment of cancer, constipation, scurvy, hemorrhoids, liver problems, boils and to increase energy, stamina and endurance. Figs kill roundworms and aid digestion, too.

Garlic

This is my favorite. I could write volumes on the medicinal uses of this astonishing herb, but suffice it to say, everyone should find SOME way to add it to their diet. Garlic fights infection, thins the blood, reduces blood pressure, prevents cancer, guards against heart disease and stimulates the immune system.

Grapes

Grapes contain compounds that thwart ruses, block cancers and even fight tooth decay. They are chock full of vitamins and nutrients essential to good health. An extract derived from grape seeds is one of the most powerful antioxidants known to man.

Honey

It kills bacteria, disinfects wounds and sores, relieves symptoms of asthma and sore throats, calms jittery nerves, promotes deep restful sleep, relieves diarrhea, boosts energy and even, like morphine, reduces the perception of pain.

Mint

This plant is a peerless digestive aid. It also has calming, relaxing, pain killing effects. Mints of any kind are good decongestants, reliable in the treatment of sinus problems and infection prevention. In addition, it is used on wounds, and burns.

Olive Oil

Olive oil actually prevents heart disease, leading one researcher to declare it "humanity's best health oil." It also lowers blood pressure and is an exceptionally rich source of vitamin E, which combats cancers, arthritis and diabetes. The oil is excellent for skin, and a simple nightly massage can reverse hair loss in men and women when pattern baldness - the genetic kind - isn't to blame. A mainstay of the heart-healthy "Mediterranean Diet" people are always talking about.

Onion

A super infection fighter and more, the onion is known to lower elevated cholesterol levels, lower high blood pressure and even ease the sugar "spiking" and related symptoms of diabetes. It In addition, fights asthma and cancers. Add a little onion to your diet daily for full benefits. If you can't take the taste, get capsules.

Rye

Biblical references to rye, say experts, are actually references to flax. Flax is good for the lungs and is used as a treatment for bronchitis and congestion. As a poultice, flax is used for shingles and psoriasis.

Vinegar

There are many kinds of vinegar, but we'll focus on apple cider vinegar, which has such a long history of medicinal use. Vinegar can be used topically in the treatment of acne, athlete's foot and other fungal complaints, excessive body odor, dandruff and minor burns.

Internally, vinegar fights headaches, helps clean arteries and improves circulation, burns fat, relieves the pain of sore throat, fights allergies, increases energy and improves respiration, according to folk use suggestions. Vinegar is, in fact, a tremendously beneficial addition to just about anyone's diet. If you simply can't tolerate the taste, try it in capsule form.

Walnut

The nuts themselves lower cholesterol, promoting healthy heart, but tea made from the leaves of the walnut tree has a long history of use as a skin wash, effective in the treatment of acne, psoriasis and eczema. A tea made of green walnut husks is useful in stopping diarrhea, sore throat and coughs. Black walnut hull is legendary for eliminating intestinal parasites.

Now these are just a few of God's many herbs and food for healing available to us when we need to live healthy, especially when medical help is not available. I want to reemphasize that these suggestions were passed down through the ages from one generation to another and not intended to prescribe health treatments.

Medical Advisory: Herbs are wondrous gifts from God but don't be foolish. If you are sick or suspect you might be, consult a healthcare professional before treating yourself or changing your diet in any significant way. The herbs and traditional uses discussed in this book are published for informational purposes and historical perspective and are not intended to diagnose, sell, treat, prevent or cure any disease.

Get rid of the TV and read more

The next step is to heal the mind. In order to heal the mind is to get rid of the TV and read more. Ever since the networks have been allowed to show sex and violence along with cuss words the minds of our youth as well as most of us have gone into the sewer.

Look at some of the religious organizations that don't allow TVs to be used as part of their religious way of life. They have less violence, have a better relationship with God and are more able to survive off the fruits of their own labor. And that's what this book is all about, helping yourself to get on the road to self-reliance and good health.

Chapter 4

Can we survive without

supermarkets?

The answer to this question is hard to say, because most of us have never had to. I would say let's hope we never have to find out. Should food supplies run out at the supermarkets, we will need a backup plan. I remember seeing news stories years ago when the food market shelves in Russia were all empty. Things were so bad they even had to pay their military with heads of cabbage gathered from the fields. Russia was not the only country with food problems.

I had an uncle, my father's brother-in-law, who while living and working in Poland was a farm produce agent for the government. His job was to go to each farm and tell the owner of the land how much food they had to produce for the government as their property tax. Anything left over was theirs to keep for themselves. That's how hard it was to produce enough food to feed the nation.

In order for many of the local farmers to survive, they had to sell or trade their goods on the black market. If they tried to do business on the open market, ruthless government officials would often come and take what they wanted for themselves without paying for it. Let's hope nothing like that ever comes to pass here in this country.

When the public food supplies in our markets are all dried up, we need to find other means of providing food for our families.

Consider homesteading

As I indicated in the preface of this book, my family and I are making an effort to do something about our health and well-being. We may not always be able to depend on commerce to provide all our basic essentials. So we believe that homesteading, or if you like, small farming, is the best way to be prepared for what may eventually come our way. We are also thinking of our health safety against the dangers of chemical poisoning in our market foods. So in the meantime, when shopping, we always read the labels to see what is in it before purchasing what we need. What we look for are the processing chemicals used in packaging.

When most people today hear the word "homesteading" they picture in their minds, covered wagons heading west from the east coast looking for a piece of land to settle on. Today, the term represents living in the country on a small piece of land where you can grow your own food, raise your own livestock, and produce everything needed to survive. If, for some reason, you find it is impossible to leave city life but yet want some of the benefits of homesteading, I will give you some ideas in this chapter.

- Homesteading can be either on or off the grid. That means with or without public utilities. However, in order to survive when public utilities are no longer available, you will need a contingent plan for survival. We are a nation of people who enjoy everything provided for us. Therefore, when you are without electricity or water for any period of time, living off the grid is like full time camping but in a structure made for permanent living.

- This will be harder to accomplish while living in a crowded neighborhood. So for the suburbanites, consider renting a small plot of land from someone who has some to spare in the country, and start your own garden there. This may mean hauling water for your garden. If you want good food, then it will be worth it. The same goes if you try to raise chickens or goats. More about that later.

- Just as soon as you know, you can survive without supermarkets; you will be on the road to self-reliance and own a "Wee Bit Of Heaven." The feeling you get when you know you can do this is one that very few people ever experience.

Getting started

Getting started will be easier if you were to live in the country on a few acres, let's say five, of fairly good land with open areas so you don't have to do a lot of clearing. And at the same time some wooded areas for firewood and wild game to live in. All of this will become obvious as we get to develop our homestead.

If you don't already have your land to homestead to live on, I will give you some things to look for before buying or renting.

- **Land –** make sure you have enough land to accomplish all that you wish to do. Like I just said, try to get land with a small amount of trees on it. If the property you get backs up against public wooded land, you will need fewer trees on your land, as long as you have permission to access your neighbors land. However, if we feel the need for survival, rather than just living in the country, having access to a wooded area is important. You can cut old and fallen trees for firewood. Wild game will have a place to live and provide for their needs. Should your food resources run out, you would have an alternate source of food as long as you are able to hunt for or trap game animals.

- **Water** – is the staple of life. Our bodies are made up of about 60 to 75% water. Without water for three days, we may die from dehydration. If your water supply should no longer be available, what back-up plan do you have? You can only store just so much for personal use, and that does not leave any to keep your garden growing. If the property you acquire has a river, stream, or a good well, then you have a better chance to make it when the public water system is turned off.

  If your property doesn't have a pond on it, consider digging one for various reasons. If your pond can be spring fed, it will keep itself filled all year long. If it is located in a low-lying area, as it should

be, you may find surface water flowing
to it or even underground water near the
surface to keep it filled.

A pond helps to keep livestock watered.
Try putting catfish in it as a continual
food source needed for good health.

- **Housing** – is the next important subject
in getting started with your homesteading. When shopping around, the newer
homes may not have as much upkeep
and repairs, but it may not be what you
need. I mention this point because many
new homes are built on cement slabs or
over a crawl space. This does not leave
any place for much storage of food and a
place to go in case of an impending disaster, such as a tornado or hurricane.
An unheated cellar may stay cool when
the temperatures outside are very hot.
You can build in your basement a vegetable and fruit room out of concrete
blocks. In addition, newer homes are
totally dependent on public utilities for
heating. The older built farmhouses generally have fireplaces or wood-burning
stoves for heat. If necessary, you could
cook from them if your gas or electricity
is no longer available.

Try to find a house with large pantries

for storage of food supplies. Your canning of your fruits and vegetables will need a cool dry place to keep them from spoiling or losing their natural color.

• **Utilities** – may be here today and gone tomorrow. Many off the grid homesteaders aren't going to wait for that to happen. They build their own utility system. For electricity, they will invest in windmills, solar panels, or generators. Generators are only good as long as fuel to run them will be available. My father-in-law once built a getaway home off the grid and installed propane gas lamps for lighting, heating, and cooking. Again, this is great as long as the propane trucks can get to you or are still in business. If you don't want to depend on anyone, then invest in the wind and/or solar forms of energy.

These forms of energy can get pricey, but if you want the comfort that you may be use to, then you may not have any choice. Remember, God has provided some natural means of energy in the form of bees wax candles and wood for heating and cooking. This is like a step back in time to our ancestors, but if they could do it, so can we.

- **Out-buildings** – can include barns, storage sheds, shelters for your animals, and
  coops for your chickens. Some of these
  items may be already there when you
  move in and what isn't should be built
  as soon as you need them. You will need
  someplace to keep your equipment out
  of the elements. It must be big enough
  to do repairs during the winter when
  your growing season is over. You need
  someplace to store your grain, hay, and
  animal feed away from the elements. The
  livestock and poultry need some place
  to keep dry and out of the elements also.
  Everyone will come up with different
  ways of providing these needs, so plan
  carefully how this is to be done.

Livestock, vegetables, and fruit trees

Not necessarily in this order, but three of the
most important aspects of homesteading:

- **Food** – production will become a challenge for those who can't live without the
  supermarkets. You can buy and store
  just so much food before it runs out, and
  then what are you going to do? The only
  answer is having something to trade for
  food from someone else. Money may or
  may not be what they will take for some-

thing that you need. In most cases, that something is also necessary for survival. If you have toilet paper and someone else has corn, you may be able to make a swap. Beyond that, the only other alternative is producing your own food and supplying your own needs. This is the time to decide what type and kind of food you can live on and not what you may desire. If you can't live without your daily cappuccino from Starbucks, then you are in trouble if you can't get coffee beans or grow them yourself.

- **Planting fruit trees** – for your future needs. This is something you need to begin as soon as possible. If your property doesn't already have fruit trees on it, then that should be the first thing you need to get started on. Most nursery purchased trees will take at least 2 to 4 years before you can expect a crop from them. As I suggest certain varieties of trees, consider purchasing trees grafted together with multiple types of the same fruits. You can buy one tree that will produce on one tree trunk three different types of apples. The same goes for pears, etc. Just shop around and you will be amazed at what nurseries have to offer.

  1. I would suggest at least 3 to 4 va-

rieties of fruit trees for beginning homesteading. Two to three varieties of apples, some early producing and another later producing. Apples are good for your health and keep well. A cold storage place can keep them most of the winter. You can make cider that keeps well until turning into apple cider vinegar or even wine.

2. Another type of tree could be a hardy peach tree that will do well in most areas. Peaches can be made into jams, canned, eaten fresh and put in all types of cooking.

3. Next could be one or two kinds of pears. I suggest one soft and one hard type. They, like peaches, make a good canning and storage food for months to come when the season is long past.

4. If you feel the need for one more, try a sweet variety of a cherry tree. Everybody likes sweet cherries. There are also a lot of people that even like sour cherries for baking pies. They make great jams for the peanut butter sandwiches or morning toast. They can also be canned for use all winter long.

- **Gardening** – can wait until your second spring season, but the garden can start being prepared during the first year. There are a variety of garden styles, such as: plow, till and plant, raised beds with walking space between each row, and pot/canister planting. The pot/canister planting will allow you to move your produce to accommodate weather conditions and needs. I will share more about this method in the next chapter. The reason I said it could wait until the second Spring, is this helps you to have a good supply of compost and energy-rich soil to start with. You will need to start that as soon as you can.

  1. Decide on the size of garden your family will require. I know that everyone's needs are more than most people are prepared to grow so start with the basics. Each year of gardening you will be able to adjust the size according to your likes and dislikes.

  2. No matter what style of garden you decide on, it will take at least one year to prepare your soil and compost for best results. One of the easiest ways to start your garden space preparation this year, if you don't have all the farm equipment needed, is to use a chicken trac-

tor. I will explain more about that further down this chapter.

3. Everyone in the homesteading lifestyle knows and appreciates the wonderful benefits of a regular compost pile. By composting, we reduce our impact on the local landfill, give nutrients to the plants we grow, and improve our soil; whether it is sandy, clay, or just dry and barren. But at the same time we are told not to put weeds that have gone to seed on our compost piles or we will pay for it later. So what does the wise homesteader do? We don't want to throw weeds with seeds in our compost piles. And we definitely don't want to send them to the landfill! So how can we use these weeds to our benefit? To extract all of the nutrients and mineral compounds that they have pulled out of our soil? And how can we do this without the headache of thousands of more weeds? Keep reading.

4. Ever wonder how to grow truly magnificent vegetables with your organic gardening? The kind that leaves your neighbors scratching their heads and wondering if you are doing genetic research in your

basement, or if you collected your seeds outside a nuclear power plant? The secret is to make your own liquid fertilizer out of all those weeds and seeds that aren't going into your compost pile.

5. The concept of how to make this liquid fertilizer is simple. The weeds pull vital minerals and nutrients from the soil as they grow. Those nutrients aren't gone. They are held inside the weeds stems and leaves. That's why goats will eat them and stay healthy. We just need to get them out and return them to the soil. To do this, we need to start with a big plastic barrel. A 55-gallon size should be large enough.

6. As you pull weeds, put them into the barrel. You can use rainwater to fill the barrel half way (only half way to account for future rains filling the barrel the rest of the way) and leave it in the sun to 'brew'. After just a few weeks, the nutrients have been pulled out of the weeds, and the liquid can be used to water your veggies with a nutrient rich liquid fertilizer. This liquid is very strong and full of everything your plant needs to grow

healthy and stay organic.

7. The old weeds left in the bottom of the barrel can now be safely tossed on the compost pile that you should still be preparing for your soil. Because the seeds have been underwater for weeks and have drowned and will not sprout, you can safely compost them. If you decide to try the fully composted method, there are some tips to remember. First, locate the barrel away from the house and downwind because the odor is intense and is similar to that of raw sewage.

8. Second, do not use this sludge on your plants until fully composted, or you will burn them up much the same as you do when using green manure.

9. Third, it is easy to know when the material is fully composted. When it's NOT ready, it smells to high heaven! When it's ready to use without burning your plants, you can put your face right over the compost pile and not smell a thing. This method works well with all compost materials such as kitchen scraps, lawn clippings, and old garden plants after they have been

harvested such as tomato vines and cabbage stalks.

- The size and type of garden will be covered in the section of this book on homesteading in suburban areas in chapter 5. Everything covered in that chapter on gardening can be applied to homesteading on a larger piece of land usually isn't found in suburban living.

- **Livestock and chickens** – are a living variety of food supplies. These types of food supplies require care and feeding before you can enjoy the results of your labor. Just like your garden, proper care and knowledge will produce great results. Reading books, or doing research on the Internet, about the living food supplies you are interested in will be most beneficial. You may desire to raise chickens, rabbits, goats, or whatever.
    1. **Let's start with chickens**. Chickens can be a simple and easy addition to anyone's garden or farm. They require minimal care and provide a number of benefits. Chickens can provide humans with food in the form of eggs and meat, fertilizer in the form of manure, light cultivation through their persistent scratching of the

ground, weed and insect control through their foraging efforts, learning opportunities for young and old alike, and can even be great friends. A chicken tractor will serve to enhance and amplify these benefits. The healthiest chickens are free-range chickens because they have fresh and varying food sources along with clean living space. When free-range is not an option, a chicken tractor can provide very near free-range conditions without the risks of chickens eating your desirable plants or your pet dog eating your desirable chickens.

2. **What is a chicken tractor?** A chicken tractor is a portable part-time or full-time shelter for chickens, which provides them with continual fresh forage space (during the growing season) and provides their caretaker with the ability to control and focus their foraging and distribution of their manure. When chickens are kept in one of their moveable coops, they will prepare the ground under it as you would cultivate it in preparation for planting. They also leave behind fertilizer in their

waste products.

3. **Chicken tractors** come in all shapes and sizes and work in a variety of different situations. Most chicken tractors are homemade, and the key ingredients are nothing more than creativity and resourcefulness. In its essence, a chicken tractor is a great way to nourish happy healthy chickens, in a manner, which is easy to manage and will provide the maximum benefits to you.

Chicken Tractor without wheels

4. When designing a chicken tractor, there are many options and variables to consider. The most common chicken tractor is of the closed-top open-bottom variety. The idea is that you build a structure over the top of your chickens that provides them with shelter and protection while still allowing them access to the ground and confining them to a space enclosed on the top and sides. This can be as simple as a giant upside down "laundry basket" where the chickens spend their days and live in a permanent coop. It can also provide full-time residence if it is built with roosting space and nesting boxes. Another option is to build a completely enclosed chicken coop on wheels and provide forage space inside a temporary fence, which is placed to create a perimeter around the chicken tractor. A third option is to place a chicken coup in a central location relative to your planting area and then give your chickens access to different sections of your garden on a rotational basis.

5. **Next good food producers are goats.** There are three major types

of goats for homesteading and survival; dairy goats, meat goats, and goats that are raised for their fur or hair. There are full-size goats and miniature goats; it all depends on the size and location of your property and your ability to care for them. I personally like the Boer meat goats and dwarf dairy goats. The dwarf dairy goats eat less food, can be penned in smaller areas and even enjoyed as small pets.

6. The **Nigerian Dwarf** goat is a miniature dairy goat breed of West African ancestry. They were originally brought to the United States on ships as food for large cats such as lions. The survivors that weren't eaten originally, later lived in zoos for people to enjoy as a novelty. Nigerian Dwarf goats are popular as hobby goats due to their easy maintenance and small stature. Though not then but now are considered a dairy goat breed, according to the show association ADGA. For its size, it can produce up to 2 quarts of milk per day. This is enough for a small family. If you want more, then raise two or more goats.

7. The **Boer goat** was developed in

South Africa in the early 1900s for meat production. Their name is derived from the Dutch word "Boer" meaning farmer. The Boer goat was probably bred from the indigenous goats of the Namaqua Bushmen and the Fooku tribes, with some crossing of Indian and European bloodlines being possible. They were selected for meat rather than milk production; due to selective breeding and improvement, the Boer goat has a fast growth rate and excellent carcass qualities, making it one of the most popular breeds of meat goat in the world.

8. **Angora goats** may be the most efficient fiber producers on Earth. These makers of mohair came from and were named after Ankara (Angora before 1930), the Turkish province where they have thrived for centuries. Turkey guarded these goats against exportation until 1849 when seven does and two bucks were imported into the United States. Later, more were imported from Turkey and South Africa, the two principal mohair producers in the 19th century. However, now the United States has become one of the two biggest

producers (along with South Africa) of mohair. Although Angora goats are somewhat delicate, they grow their fleeces year-round. This puts considerable strain on the animal, and probably contributes to their lack of hardiness.

9. **What are the benefits of eating and raising rabbits**? All over the world, rabbits are raised for a variety of reasons. Some cultures raise them for food while others raise them strictly for their pelts. A rabbit is only 20 percent bone, so there is little waste when producing the animal for food. The meat is fine grained and used very similar to poultry, according to North Dakota State University. The nutritional value of rabbit has been tested thoroughly by the U.S. Department of Agriculture. Rabbit meat is about 20.8 percent protein and only contains 4.5 percent fat and 795 calories per pound. By comparison, beef is 16.3 percent protein, and chicken is about 20 percent. Another competitor to rabbit meat is veal, which contains 19.1 percent protein, but lost its impressive standing by logging 12 percent fat

North Dakota State University recommends rabbits be raised in relatively small structures that include cages with wire mesh bottoms (so the cages are "self-cleaning.") The most expensive part of raising rabbits is purchasing feed, which can be about 75 percent of the total production costs, according to North Dakota State University

Hutches can either be store bought (already assembled), bought as a kit that you put together, or built from scratch. It is advisable to build them entirely from wire mesh, which will last longer, but can be built with a wood frame if you have scrap wood lying around.

Adult rabbits need their own individual cages, and the dimensions should be at least 2ft by 2ft for each cage floor (or larger) and 18 in. high so they can stretch out. Note, regardless of the size you make the cages, ensure that you will be able to get the rabbit when you need to, if you make them too deep, they will run to the far corner out of your reach.

Look at all the health benefits

Everything thus far has been for the benefits of survival when we can no longer get our food from the supermarkets. There are even greater benefits that are most often overlooked when raising your own food and that is you have control over what goes into the food you grow for consumption. We read and hear about all the food recalls because of E. coli poisoned food. *E. coli* O157:H7 was first recognized as a food-borne pathogen in 1982 during an investigation into an outbreak of hemorrhagic colitis (bloody diarrhea) associated with the consumption of contaminated hamburgers (Riley, et al., 1983). The following year, Shiga toxin (Stx), produced by the then little-known *E. coli* O157:H7, was identified as the real culprit.

In the ten years following the 1982 outbreak, approximately thirty *E. coli* O157:H7 outbreaks were recorded in the United States (Griffin & Tauxe, 1991). The actual number that occurred is probably much higher because *E. coli* O157:H7 infections did not become a reportable disease (required to be reported to public health authorities) until 1987 (Keene et al., 1991 p. 60, 73). As a result, only the most geographically concentrated outbreaks would have garnered enough attention to prompt further investigation (Keene et al., 1991 p. 583). It is important to note that about 10 percent of infections occur in outbreaks, the rest are sporadic.

The CDC has estimated that 85 percent of *E. coli* O157:H7 infections are food-borne in origin (Mead, et al., 1999). In fact, consumption of any food or beverage that becomes contaminated by animal (especially cattle) manure can result in contracting the disease. Foods that have been identified as sources of contamination include ground beef, venison, sausages, dried (non-cooked) salami, unpasteurized milk and cheese, unpasteurized apple juice and cider (Cody, et al., 1999), orange juice, alfalfa and radish sprouts (Breuer, et al., 2001), lettuce, spinach, and water (Friedman, et al., 1999). Pizza and cookie dough has also been identified as sources of *E. coli* outbreaks.

Beyond the food poisoning scare, lets look at the other health benefits of producing our own food.

I listed in chapter 3 many of the healing herbs and vegetables, so I won't repeat them again, but I will go into the benefits of chickens, rabbits, and goats for survival and healthy living. In order to show the good of organic raised food, I will show the industry bad that you can keep out of your own food products.

In most animal produced industries, things like hormones are injected or fed to animals before being shipped to market.

What are hormones?

Hormones are chemicals that are produced naturally in the bodies of all animals, including humans. They are chemical messages released into the blood by hormone-producing organs that travel to and affect different parts of the body. Hormones may be produced in small amounts, but they control important body functions such as growth, development and reproduction.

Hormones can have different chemistry. They can be steroids or proteins. Steroid hormones are active in the body when eaten. For example, birth control pills are steroid hormones and can be taken orally. In contrast, protein hormones are broken down in the stomach, and lose their ability to act in the body when eaten. Therefore, ordinarily, protein hormones need to be injected into the body to have an effect. An example is insulin, which is a protein hormone. Diabetic patients need to be injected with insulin for treatment.

Why are hormones used in food production?

Certain hormones can make young animals gain weight faster. They help reduce the waiting time and the amount of feed eaten by an animal before slaughter in meat industries. In dairy cows, hormones can be used to increase milk production. Thus, hormones can increase the profitability of the meat and dairy industries.

Why are consumers concerned about hormones in foods?

While a variety of hormones are produced by our bodies and are essential for normal development of healthy tissues, synthetic steroid hormones used as pharmaceutical drugs, have been found to affect cancer risk. For example, diethylstilbestrol (DES), a synthetic estrogen drug used in the 1960s was withdrawn from use after it was found to increase the risk of vaginal cancer in daughters of treated women. Lifetime exposure to natural steroid hormone estrogen is also associated with an increased risk for breast cancer (see BCERF Fact Sheet #09 *Estrogen and Breast Cancer Risk: What is the Relationship?*). Hence, consumers are concerned about whether they are being exposed to hormones used to treat animals, and whether these hormones affect human health.

History of hormone use in food production

As early as the 1930s, it was realized that cows injected with material drawn from bovine (cow) pituitary glands (hormone secreting organ) produced more milk. Later, the bovine growth hormone (bGH) from the pituitary glands was found to be responsible for this effect. However, at that time, technology did not exist to harvest enough of this material for large-scale

use in animals. In the 1980s, it became possible to produce large quantities of pure bGH
by using recombinant DNA technology. In
1993, the Food and Drug Administration (FDA)
approved the recombinant bovine growth hormone (rbGH), also known as bovine somatotro-
pin (rbST) for use in dairy cattle. Recent esti-
mates by the manufacturer of this hormone
indicate that 30% of the cows in the United
States (US) may be treated with rbGH.

Need I say more about the dangers of animals
injected with hormones? So as long as you have
control over what goes into animals raised for
food, these hormone dangers are eliminated.

Chickens

There has always been the on-going fight with
the beef and poultry industries over which are
better for you. Yes, red meat has better protein for body builders, but we are not dealing
with body building in this book. We are dealing with survival and health with your own
raised animals. If you have the space and pa-
tience to wait and raise beef, then go for it.
However, most homesteaders won't have much
space, including those who are homesteading
in the city.

Chickens can be raised just about anywhere
and on a small amount of space. If there is

one word that describes a chicken, it is versatility. Roasted, broiled, grilled or poached, and combined with a wide range of herbs and spices, chicken makes a delicious, flavorful and nutritious meal. It is no wonder chicken is the world's primary source of animal protein and a healthy alternative to red meat. It is available to enjoy throughout the year.

Chicken is rated as a very good source of protein, providing 67.6% of the daily value for protein in 4 ounces. The structure of humans and animals is built on protein. We derive our amino acids from animal and plant sources of protein, and then rearrange the nitrogen to make the pattern of amino acids we require.

People who are meat eaters, but are looking for ways to reduce the amount of fat in their meals, can try eating more chicken. The leanest part of the chicken is the chicken breast, which has less than half the fat of a trimmed choice grade T-bone steak. The fat in chicken is also less saturated than beef fat. However, eating the chicken with the skin doubles the amount of fat and saturated fat in the food. For this reason, chicken is best skinned before cooking.

Chicken is a very good source of the cancer-protective B vitamin and niacin. Components of DNA require niacin, and a deficiency of niacin (as well as other B-complex vitamins) has been directly linked to genetic (DNA) damage. A four-ounce serving of chicken provides 72.0% of the daily value for niacin.

Chicken is also a good source of the trace mineral, selenium. Selenium is of fundamental importance to human health. It is an essential component of several major metabolic pathways, including thyroid hormone metabolism, antioxidant defense systems, and immune function. Accumulated evidence from prospective studies, intervention trials and studies on animal models of cancer has suggested a strong inverse correlation between selenium intake and cancer incidence.

Rabbits

As stated earlier, the nutritional value of rabbit has been tested thoroughly by the U.S. Department of Agriculture. Rabbit meat is about 20.8 percent protein and only contains 4.5 percent fat and 795 calories per pound. By comparison, beef is 16.3 percent protein, and chicken is about 20 percent. Another competitor to rabbit meat is veal, which contains 19.1 percent protein, but lost its impressive standing by logging 12 percent fat.

Back in the 1950s rabbit meat was as common for dinner as chicken is today. It is the meat that got many people and their children through the lean times of the Depression. They lost their popularity after Big AGRA, who wanted to get maximum profits with the cheapest bottom line using the government endorsed chemicals and handouts. Because of this, rabbits didn't make sense. So why rabbit meat now? Below you will find a few reasons why you should consider adding rabbit meat to your diet.

1. It is one of the best white meats available on the market today.
2. The meat has a high percentage of easily digestible protein.
3. It contains the least amount of fat among all the other available meats.
4. Rabbit meat contains less caloric value than other meats.
5. Rabbit meat is almost cholesterol free and therefore, heart healthy.
6. The sodium content of rabbit meat is comparatively less than other meats.
7. The calcium and phosphorus contents of this meat are higher than any other meats.
8. The ratio of meat to bone is high, meaning, there is more edible meat on the carcass than even a chicken.
9. Rabbit meat with the many health

> benefits does not have a strong flavor and is comparable to chicken but not identical.
> 10. Rabbits are one of the most productive domestic livestock animals, there is.
> 11. Rabbits can produce 6 pounds of meat on the same feed and water as the cow, who will produce 1 pound of meat.

So as you can see there are many health benefits to eating rabbit meat. It is healthy for you and cheap to produce.

Goats

Types of goat meat
Rather than identifying and purchasing goat meat by the cut, such as pork ribs or rump roast, consumers generally purchase goat meat according to the age of the animal at the time of slaughter and typically buy whole or half carcasses. Cabrito, considered a delicacy in Central and South America, comes from goats no more than three months old that weighed less than 50 lb. at the time of slaughter. Chevon is the meat from goats that were 6 to 9 months of age and weighed between 50 and 75 lb. at slaughter. Mature goat meat comes from animals above one year of age.

Nutrients in Goat Meat

A 3 oz. serving of cooked goat meat contains fewer calories than the same cooked weight of beef, chicken, lamb or pork: 122 calories in goat meat vs. 162 in chicken, 179 in beef, 180 in pork and 175 in lamb.

Goat meat has 2.6 g of total fat, 0.79 g of saturated fat, 63.8 mg of cholesterol and 23 g of protein per 3 oz. serving. It also has relatively high levels of iron compared to its competitors, 3.2 mg per 3 oz. serving vs. 2.9 mg in beef, 2.7 mg in pork, 1.4 mg in lamb and 1.5 mg in chicken. Goat meat is also a rich source of potassium.

Health Benefits

Goat meat provides a leaner protein source than beef, lamb, chicken or pork. This means it is low in saturated fat, the type that increases your LDL cholesterol, and higher in unsaturated fats, the type that helps increase your HDL, or good cholesterol. The American Heart Association recommends you include leaner meats such as goat to help decrease your risk of heart disease, stroke and other serious medical conditions.

Considerations

The lack of fat in goat meat means it needs a low temperature and moisture, such as a marinade, to keep it from drying out or becoming tough during cooking. The meat from goat kids, cabrito and chevon, are good options for recipes that call for stewed, baked or grilled meat. Mature goat meat works well when ground and used in sausage, chili and other processed foods.

Goat Milk vs. Cow Milk

- Nutrient content of goat milk is slightly less than cow milk but goat milk is more digestible because the fat molecules are one-fifth the size of those from cow milk, making it easily tolerated by those with compromised digestive systems.
- Seventy-two percent of the milk used throughout the world is from goats. It is one-third richer than cow's milk but more nourishing and easier to digest.
- The flavor of goat milk is comparable to that of cow milk. Goat milk has a milder taste.
- Goat milk has no cream separation because of smaller fat molecules.
- Goat milk contains pre-formed Vitamin A in the milk fat that allows it to be readily available for use by the body.
- Goat milk contains more highly evolved cholesterol than cow's milk, making it more available for absorption to the brain and body. (Cholesterol is essential to the

health of the myelin sheaths "white matter" of the nerves in the brain.)

- Goat milk is closer to human milk and is therefore easily accepted especially by those young or frail.
- Goat milk has an alkaline reaction the same as mother's milk. Cow milk has an acid reaction.
- Goat milk does not form mucous (phlegm) and is therefore better tolerated by asthmatics and those with allergies.
- Goat milk contains more chlorine, fluorine and silicon than any other domestic livestock. Chlorine and fluorine are natural germicides, and fluorine assists in preventing diabetes.
- Goat milk contains 2% curd, which precipitates in the stomach. Cow's milk is 10% curd.
- Goats are naturally immune to diseases, such as tuberculosis, and are used in third-world countries to actually cure tuberculosis because of their inherent antibodies.
- Goat milk is tolerated by a compromised or damaged liver because of the smaller fat molecules, and it's naturally homogenized.
- Goat milk has the ability to "sweeten" the intestinal tract and assist with constipation.

- Goat milk contains a higher evolved caro-
  tene (pro-Vitamin A). Researchers have
  found this to have cancer-preventing
  properties.

If we never have to homestead for natural disasters or economic failure, just changing our
way of eating and what we eat will keep you
and your family healthy. It is not an impossible task to undertake when it comes to your
health.

Storing and processing what you pro-
duce

When it comes to storing what you produce, it
will depend on how you process what you want
to store.

Storing your fresh fruits and vegetables

Harvesting fruits and vegetables from your garden at the right stage of maturity is only the
first step to fresh table quality. Proper harvesting and post-harvest handling methods, as well
as proper storage of fruits and vegetables, will
help maintain the flavor, texture and nutritive
value of the produce.

Proper storage means controlling both the temperature and relative humidity of the storage
area. All fruits and vegetables do not have the

same requirements. I will help you select the best storage conditions for homegrown and purchased produce.

To clean or not to clean before storage

Most fruits and vegetables are easily bruised when not handled carefully. When harvesting, treat produce as if it were fine china. Tossing fruits and vegetables into baskets or boxes may not leave visible bruises and damage, but decay will begin under the skin. Seemingly sturdy vegetables such as sweet potatoes are actually quite tender and will not store well if bruised.

Not all produce should be washed upon harvest. Berries, for example, are very delicate and fragile. Rinse them in cold water just before consuming, as prior washing will cause them to break down and turn mushy. Potatoes store better if they have a fine layer of soil left on the skin to reduce moisture loss and prevent the infestation of water-borne bacteria or fungi. Water can transport bacteria and fungi into the pores of fruits and vegetables as well, reducing viable storage time.

Some produce, however, is washed and dried before storing. Commercial packing houses use sanitizers in packing lime water to kill the fungi, bacteria and yeast that might otherwise cause spoilage. Sodium hypochlorite (liquid laundry bleach) is the most readily available of these sanitizers. Excessive use of hypochlorite can result in off-flavors, tissue damage and may change the surface pH of the produce, encouraging microbial growth. Therefore, it is important to use only the recommended amount of bleach in the wash water when cleaning produce.

Curing vegetables to improve shelf-life
Several vegetables benefit from post-harvest curing. Curing heals injuries from harvesting operations. It thickens the skin, reducing moisture loss and affording better protection against insect and microbial invasion. Curing is usually accomplished at an elevated storage temperature and high humidity.

Produce can be cured in home storage areas. Temperature and humidity should be managed as accurately as possible. A space heater in an enclosed area can provide the needed heat for curing. Overlying containers with sheets of plastic can increase humidity.

Root crops such as beets, carrots, rutabagas, parsnips and turnips can be left in the garden into late fall and early winter. A heavy mulch of straw will help prevent the ground from freezing so the roots can be dug when needed. The mulch will also maintain the quality of the roots, as it will reduce repeated freezing and thawing of the vegetables. Many people prefer the taste of these root crops after they have been frosted because their flavors become sweeter and milder.

When temperatures drop low enough to freeze the ground under the mulch, finish harvesting the roots. Cut off all but one-half-inch of the leafy top and store at 32° to 40°F in high humidity to reduce shriveling.

Handling of specific vegetables and fruits

Irish Potatoes — Late-crop potatoes are better for long-term storage than early potatoes since outdoor temperatures are usually lower when they are harvested. After the harvest, cure late potatoes by holding them in moist air for 1 to 2 weeks at 60 to 75°F. Wounds will not heal at 50°F or below. When you are done curing, lower the storage temperature to about 40-45°F. Potatoes will keep even longer at 35-40°F but at 35°F, potatoes tend to become sweet. This condition can be corrected by holding the potatoes at about 70°F for a week or two before you use them.

Potatoes will keep well for several months in a cool basement or cellar. They keep best in moderately moist air, which helps prevent shriveling. Do not wash potatoes before they are put into storage.

Onions can be harvested when the tops have

fallen over and begun to dry. Do not bend the tops over during the growing season to "force the energy into the bulb." This practice reduces the growth of the onions, as they will not be able to translocate sugars to the bulb for storage.

Commercially, onions are dug, windrowed and allowed to cure in the field before they are picked up. Home gardeners should cure onions after harvest by spreading them in a single layer on screens in the shade or in a well-ventilated garage or shed for 1 to 2 weeks or until the tops are completely dry and shriveled. If the bulbs are exposed to full sun, prevent sunscald by covering with a lightweight cloth. When the tops are dry, they should be trimmed to 1-inch lengths. Leave the onion's dry outer skins on; they help reduce bruising and shrinking and act as an insect barrier.

Store onions in shallow boxes, mesh bags or hang them in old nylons in a cold, dry, well-ventilated room. The tops may be left untrimmed and braided together. Temperatures close to 32°F will give the longest storage. Products prone to absorb odors or flavors should not be stored close to onions.

Sweet and hot peppers — Mature green bell peppers can be kept for 2 or 3 weeks if handled properly. Firm, dark-green peppers free of blemishes and injury are best for storage.

To prevent chilling injury, pick peppers just before frost or before frost threatens if daytime temperatures are consistently below 45°F. Wash them with water containing 1 1/2 tsp. of chlorine bleach per gallon of water. Then dry and sort according to maturity and firmness. Store peppers in boxes lined with plastic or in plastic bags that have several 1/4" holes punched in them to maintain high humidity. The temperature should be between 45 and 50°F. Fully mature green peppers may turn red during storage.

Hot chili peppers are easiest to store after they are dry. One exception is habanero or Scotch bonnet type peppers. These do not dry well except in a dehydrator. Both pulling the plants and hanging them upside down or by picking the peppers from the plants and stringing together can dry peppers. Ripe chili peppers can be dried in a forced-air dehydrator, but it is usually not necessary to do so.

Tomatoes — With care, mature green tomatoes will keep and ripen for about 4 to 6 weeks in the fall. Some cultivars have been developed for even longer storage. Tomatoes from nearly spent vines are more subject to decay and are usually not as good quality as those from vigorous vines. A late planting of tomatoes will provide vigorous vines from which fruit can be harvested for storage.

Harvest tomatoes just before the first killing frost. If an unexpected frost occurs, undamaged fruits can be salvaged and ripened. Prevent chilling injury to the fruit by harvesting everything when temperatures drop regularly from 32° to 50°F.

To store, pick the tomatoes and remove the stems. Reduce rots by disinfecting fruits by washing in water with 1 1/2 teaspoon of chlorine bleach per gallon of water. Dry thoroughly with a soft cloth.

Pack tomatoes 1 or 2 layers deep in shallow boxes. Reduce bruising by separating those showing red; they will ripen sooner and can be used first.

Pumpkins and winter squash — Harvest mature fruit with hard rinds before frost. Leave the stem on when cutting from the plants to prevent decay organisms from entering. Pumpkins and winter squash will keep best if they are cured for 10 days at 80-85°F. Acorn squash, however, should not be cured but stored at 45°F to prevent stringiness.

Apples — Many cultivars of apples store moderately well under home storage conditions for up to six months. Late maturing varieties are best suited to storage. These apples can be stored in baskets or boxes lined with plastic or foil to help retain moisture. Always sort apples carefully to avoid bruising them. The saying "one bad apple spoils the barrel" is true because apples give off ethylene gas, which speeds ripening. When damaged, ethylene is given off more rapidly and will hasten the ripening of other apples in the container. Because of their sugar content, apples can be stored at 30-32°F without freezing the tissue. In general, apples ripen about four times as fast at 50°F as at 32°F, so they should be kept as close to 32°F as possible for long-term storage.

Apples often pass their odor or flavor to more delicately flavored produce and the ethylene given off by apples can accelerate ripening in other crops. When possible, store apples separately.

Pears — For good flavor and texture, pears, except for 'Seckel' must be ripened after harvest. Pick pears when they are fully mature. Fruit is ready to harvest while it is quite firm, but the color has lightened to a pale green. It should part easily from the branch when you lift up on the fruit and twist. Pears left to ripen on the tree tend to become grainy or stringy. The center also may turn brown before the exterior shows deterioration.

Pears ripen quickly after harvest when held at 60 to 65°F. Ripening will take 1 to 3 weeks, depending on the type of pear. After ripening, pears should be canned or preserved. To keep pears longer in storage, sort for defects after picking and place sound fruit into cold storage at 29-31°F and 90% humidity. Ripen small amounts as needed, by moving them to a warmer location, 60-65°F. Too high of temperatures (75°F and higher) will cause the fruit to break down without ripening.

Canning fresh fruits and vegetables

One of the best things about early fall is being able to can the fruits and vegetables from your garden so you can enjoy them all winter long.

The basic principle is simple: during the canning process, food is heated to a high enough temperature to stop the decaying action of enzymes and/or bacteria and other critters in the food. The food is then stored in sterile, airtight containers to keep it from spoiling.

Even though the process is pretty straightforward, you still have to pay attention. Contaminated food can cause illness, and botulism isn't something you want to mess with. Here are some tips to give you the best results when canning:

- Choose only the best produce. Overripe

or damaged fruits and vegetables are more prone to spoilage.

- Jars, lids and sealing rings should be in good condition and sterile (washed and scalded).
- Wash produce thoroughly before processing. Be sure to use the correct time, temperature and method of processing for the food you will be canning. Use a reputable source like The Ball Blue Book.
- After canning, check the seal on every jar to make sure they are air tight. When you push down on a self-sealing lid, it should stay down. Test porcelain lids by turning the jars upside down. If you see a stream of tiny air bubbles, the seal is not airtight.
- Don't use foods from any jar that has a foamy or discolored appearance. Watch for bulging or misshapen lids and leaking rims. Throw those jars away. Glass jars used for home canning usually have a self-sealing cap, which consists of a flat lid with sealant around the rim and a screw-on band that holds the lid against the lip of the jar. The band can be re-used, but you should use a new lid for each process.
- Vegetables and large fruits can be cut into pieces and pitted if necessary. Smaller fruits such as berries can be left

whole. Fruits can be dipped in ascorbic acid (vitamin C) and packed in sugar syrup to preserve their color, texture and flavor.

There are two ways to pack the produce into the jars before processing: raw or cooked. For raw packed, place clean produce tightly into containers and pour on boiling juice, water or syrup. Wipe the rim and sealing ring to remove any food particles, then close the jar and proceed with the canning process. For hot packed, steam or heat vegetables or fruits to boiling in juice, water or syrup, then immediately pack them into the jars. If you are using a self-sealing cap jar, tighten band before processing and don't loosen it again.

So far, we've covered the initial steps of selection and preparation. Now we'll take a look at the two types of canning and cover the rest of the steps you'll need to make your own delicious pickles and preserves.

There are two also ways to can fruits and vegetables: boiling-water bath or pressure canning. All vegetables (except tomatoes) can contain heat-resistant bacteria, and MUST be pressure canned. High acid food, which includes tomatoes, pickled vegetables and most fruits, can be processed at boiling water temperature.

Energy efficient steam canner

An energy-efficient steam canner can be purchased at most canning supply stores. This method, like the boiling method below, use water to a boiling point for its preserving process with equipment a little different. This method doesn't insert the bottles directly into the water but on a rack above it. Everything else works the same.

For boiling-water bath canning, you'll need:

1. Boiling-water bath canner. This is basically a large, deep pan with a tight-fitting lid. It should be large enough to allow 4 or more inches of "headroom" above the jars.
2. Wire basket or rack to fit inside the pan and hold your jars.
3. Tongs to lift jars out of boiling water.
4. Oven mitts to handle hot jars.
5. Cooling rack, or several towels.
6. Kitchen timer.

To start, fill the canner halfway with hot water and put the jars, lids and rings in it. Add boiling water to 2 inches above the jars. Be careful not to pour boiling water directly onto the jars.

Cover canner tightly and bring water to a rolling boil for 5 minutes to sterilize the jars.

When time is up, remove jars, lids and rings

immediately with the tongs. Fill the jars according to the recipe, place the lids and rings on, and place the jars in the canner. Bring the water back to a boil and process for the time called for in the recipe.

For pressure canning, you will need:
1. Pressure canner with an accurate dial or gauge
2. Rack to fit inside the canner
3. Tongs to lift jars out of boiling water
4. Oven mitts to handle hot jars
5. Cooling rack, or several towels
6. Kitchen timer

Fill the pressure canner with 2-3 inches of hot water and put the jars on a rack on the bottom of the pan. Jars should be spaced apart from each other. Fasten the lid and place over a maximum heat. Let steam exhaust for 10 minutes. When the first inch of the steam jet is nearly invisible, close the vent. At 8 pound pressure, lower heat slightly. Let the pressure continue to rise to 10 pounds. At 10 pound pressure, start timing. Hold at that pressure for the full canning period. (Use a chart available where you purchased your canner to determine processing time.) If pressure drops below 10 pounds at any time during the process, start timing all over again. Remove canner from heat and let it cool. (Don't pour cold water on it.) When the pressure is zero, open the vent, and then carefully open the lid, slanting it away from you. Set the jars on a cooling rack or layer of towels to cool, leaving spaces between the jars. Tighten lids if necessary.

After canning, label the jars with their contents and the date when they were canned. Store jars in a cool, dark place. Light can cause discoloration and loss of nutrients.

This chapter was much longer than I planned on, but as I developed it, I felt all this information was necessary to show that in many ways we can, if necessary, survive without supermarkets. Like I said at the beginning of this chapter, I hope we never have to find out. Even so, again if you are interested in the quality of food, your family eats, then try incorporating many of these ideas.

Chapter 5

City and suburban

self reliance

Most of what I talked about in chapter 4 can be applied to city or suburban living. Yes out in the country you have more land and even streams and forests, but it doesn't mean you can't become self-reliant in small spaces. My orthopedic surgeon whom I mentioned in the preface of this book has a home with one and one half acres of land. When I told him about the subject mater of this book, he said a friend of his was coming from Tennessee to help him put in a garden for some of his family's needs and healthy living. This is going to be a new experience for him, and he is willing to give it a try for the good of his family.

Time to be creative

Living in smaller spaces means you will have

to be a little creative in how you use what you have. For example, do you want to have the ability to grow your own organic vegetables? If you do, there are different ways you can accomplish this task and have all you want to eat. I will go over various types of gardening to grow plenty of veggies in small spaces.

Square foot gardening
Square foot gardening is a clever approach to growing food. It's easy to do, easy to manage, very adaptable, and it produces high yields of top-quality food. There are two types of square foot gardening; the raised bed and the in-ground. This will depend on your likes and dislikes.

Let's start with the in-ground first. One square foot garden units measuring 16 sq ft (1.5 sq meters) holds an average of 130 plants and produces enough vegetables for one person. A family of four can have fresh greens in abundance throughout the growing season and beyond from only 64 sq ft of growing space (6 sq meters).

If you have a garden, but you're no expert, or new to growing food, first choose a good site. So you ask, "What makes a good site?" Lots of sunshine, and lots and lots of that "well-drained, rich, loamy soil". The type the seed packets tell you to plant your seeds in, as if the stuff grows on trees. So just choose a good place where there's enough light. You will be able to fix the soil to your needs.

Take up a bit of lawn if you like, the soil under a lawn is usually quite good. Use a sharp spade to cut through the turf: make vertical cuts (use your foot), slicing it up into one-foot squares, then peel the squares off like a carpet. You only need to take off a couple of inches. Pile the squares in a block, grass-side down, wet thoroughly as you go, cover the top with a garbage bag to keep it moist, and it will rot into a useful supply of well-drained, rich, loamy soil.

This is the most time-consuming part of the whole process. Some folks just spray some herbicide on the grass and build their raised bed over it. I prefer to increase the drainage by removing the sod.

If you have some suitable garden space with fairly good soil you've been using for growing, use that. If all you have is some rough, hard ground, don't despair; it will do, with a bit more trouble. Put some pegs in the ground and use string to mark where the beds will be (include a 15" path space around the beds), and then cover with a thick layer of hay, grass clippings, dead leaves. Anything that'll make a good mulch. Make it at least six inches thick; if it sinks, add more. Keep it well watered, and don't let anyone walk on it. After a few weeks, the ground will be much softer. Scoop off the mulch (you can use it later in the garden or in the compost), and you can begin.

If you want to get started right away without waiting for your garden to go through what was suggested above, then there is the quick, lazy way. You can "grow" fertile soil from the top down. First build wooden sides and ends for your beds, about 10-12 inches high. Then put compost in, straight onto the ground, to a depth of at least 6 inches, preferably more. Go right ahead and plant. You'll have great crops from the start.

Keep adding more compost on top as the surface sinks. The plant roots will steadily penetrate the soil below, and worms will mysteriously appear even if there didn't seem to be any before, all doing your deep digging for you.

Before too long the soil will be soft, deep and fertile. Just keep adding compost. There's no such thing as too much compost. This method is called the raised bed gardening. The original raised square foot unit is 4x4 ft, 16 sq ft, which can supply one person with vegetables and salads. Many gardeners have found this square block harder to work with when you have to reach into, in order to pull weeds or gather crops. Many people now use 3x3 ft beds instead, which works well, with good access all around. 3x3 ft seems to have become the standard size for school gardens using the square foot system. If this size does not provide enough food for your needs, then build a second or third box.

Container gardening

No ground at all? High-rise living? There's still a lot you can do. You can have a small square foot garden on a balcony or patio. You can grow plants in virtually anything that holds some soil and has holes in the bottom for drainage. It's only bounded by your imagination — a chance for some really creative recycling.

A windowsill, a patio, a balcony or a doorstep will provide sufficient space for a productive mini-garden. Problems with soil borne diseases, nematodes or poor soil conditions can be easily overcome by switching to a container garden. Ready access to containers means that pest management is easier. Container vegetable gardening is a sure way to introduce children to the joys and rewards of vegetable gardening.

Containers

Almost any type of container can be used for growing vegetable plants. For example, try using bushel baskets, drums, gallon cans, tubs or wooden boxes. The size of the container will vary according to the crop selection and space available. Pots from 6 to 10 inches in size are satisfactory for green onion, parsley and herbs. For most vegetable crops such as tomatoes, peppers and eggplant, you will find that 5-gallon containers are a more suitable size, while 1 to 2-gallon containers are best for chard and dwarf tomatoes. Smaller container sizes are appropriate for herbs, lettuce, and radish crops. They are fairly easy to handle and provide adequate space for root growth.

Container materials are either porous or non-porous. Glazed, plastic, metal, and glass containers are nonporous. Regardless of the type or size of the container used, it must drain adequately for successful yields. Adding about 1 inch of coarse gravel in the bottom of the container will improve drainage. The drain holes work best when they are located along the side of the container, about ¼ to ½ inch from the bottom.

Soil and fertilizers

You can use soil in your container vegetable garden made from an equal mixture of sand, loamy garden soil and peat moss, but potting mixes are much better. Peat-based mixes, containing peat and vermiculite, are excellent. They are relatively sterile and pH adjusted. They also allow the plants to get enough air and water. Mixing in one part compost to two parts planting mix will improve fertility. Using a slow release or complete organic fertilizer at planting will keep your vegetables fed for the whole growing season.

Watering

Pots and containers always require more frequent watering than plants in the ground. As the season progresses and your plants mature, their root system will expand and require even more water. Don't wait until you see the plants wilting. Check your containers daily to judge the need for water.

Seeding and transplanting

Vegetables that can be easily transplanted are best suited for container culture. Vegetable transplants may be purchased from local nurseries or can be grown at home. Seeds can also be germinated in a baking pan, plastic tray, pot, or even a cardboard milk carton. Fill the container with the media described above and cover most vegetable seeds with ¼ inch to ½ inch of media to ensure good germination. Another method is to use peat pellets or peat pots, which are available from nursery supply centers. Landscape cloth or screen in the bottom of the pot will improve drainage and invigorate plant growth.

Any well-drained container can become a productive mini-garden. Green onions, radishes or beets can be grown in a cake pan. The seed should be started in a warm area that receives sufficient sunlight about 4 to 8 weeks before you plan to transplant them into the final container. Most vegetables should be transplanted into containers when they develop their first two to three true leaves. Transplant the seedlings carefully to avoid injuring the young root system.

Plants that work well in containers
Almost any vegetable that will grow in a typical backyard garden will also do well as a container-grown plant. Vegetables that are ideally suited for growing in containers include tomatoes, peppers, eggplant, green onions, beans, lettuce, squash, radishes and parsley. Pole beans and cucumbers also do well in this type of garden, but they do require considerably more space because of their vining growth habit.

Seed companies realize that homeowners have less and less space to devote to vegetable gardens. Every year they come out with new vegetable plant varieties suitable for growing in small spaces and vegetable container gardens. Be on the look out for key words like: bush, compact, and space saver.

Raising chickens inside city limits

Most cities will allow chickens to be raised inside city limits but I suggest you don't raise any roosters. Your neighbors might complain and give you a hard time. Broilers and laying hens don't make enough noise to bother anybody. If you keep them in small portable coops (like the chicken tractor), you can move them around to soot you desires.

Raising chickens
Raising chickens in your backyard in the city or suburbs is a good way to build community acceptance by sharing some of your eggs with your neighbors. The fresh eggs are a great food source and taste much better than a store bought egg!

If you don't already, you will need to know what to do through the various stages of the chicken's life.

Starting in the early spring, you can find baby chicks at your local feed stores. They are may be just a few days old when they first arrive. The feed store suppliers are usually able to sex the chicks and provide mainly hens for laying eggs. They do this by examining the shape of the egg. This process is about 95% accurate. Most shops will let you bring the roosters back. The mortality rate is high in baby chicks as they are fragile. Be prepared to lose one to unknown causes. Chances are you can buy one more than you need. Sexing Bantams is more difficult, and you may end up with roosters. Ask your feed store if they are sexed before hatching. They will have a better idea of what your chances are of getting hens or roosters.

What kind of chickens do you want?

There are several breeds of chickens that lay white eggs. Some lay extremely well, while others are very poor layers. If you have decided to keep a small flock of backyard chickens, this information may help you decide on which type of chicken to raise.

The egg color is indicative of the type of chicken. Certain breeds lay different color eggs. For instance, Black Beauty hens lay pale brown eggs. The Aracuna lays colored eggs ranging from olive green to turquoise. Eggshell pigment color is genetic in much the same way skin color is.

White Leghorn chickens are at the top of the list for laying huge quantities of large, white eggs. Their feathers are solid white in color. They are of a small body type, so are unsuitable for supplying fresh meat. If you intend to keep them confined, they will probably need an enclosed area with a fence over the top, as they tend to be flighty. They are a hardy breed and do well in temperature extremes.

As near as I can tell, there are few other differences between eggs. Some people say that different color eggs taste differently, but most farmers assert that taste is entirely dependent on what the chicken eats, and egg color has nothing to do with it. Though there is a myth that brown eggs are more nutritious than white, there is no difference in nutritional value between the two.

Meat chickens, sometimes known as fryers or broilers, are grown for their meat. If meat is what you want from your flock, then size, weight, and appearances are the primary factors. Some good meat chickens like the New Hampshire (an offshoot of the Rhode Island) can grow up to 9 pounds. In addition, skin color and "dress ability" become factors for chickens bred for eating.

Dual-purpose chickens are egg layers early in life, and as their production slows, they are fattened up for meat. If you want eggs and meat, the dual-purpose bird is the way to go. Find out what your local feed store has to start with. Your choices may be limited by what is available. You can spend a lot of time doing research about what kind to get.

Feeding/Watering-
Chicks need starter feed that is usually high protein. Most starter feeds have antibiotics in them. I am not sure if a small backyard flock really needs this, but that is what a lot of feed stores offer. It is because chicks are prone to diseases such as coccidiosis.

You can also put a little sugar in their water (approx. 1-tablespoon) when they are just a few days old to give them more energy.

Some little ones may need to learn to drink water. Just dip their beaks into the water to encourage drinking. The water often has to be changed daily at this stage, as they tend to push the shavings around and into the water. It is a good idea to lift the water and food containers off the ground level to reduce the amount of shavings, bedding and debris that get in the water.

Buy a big metal garbage can with a lid that is secure (or make it secure with a bungee cord over the top) to store the food in and keep out critters. (Mice can chew through the plastic garbage cans.)

Housing
Chicks need a warm, contained area like a big box or crate. The temperature needs to be kept at 90 degrees for the first week and can be reduced by 5 degrees every week until they are about 4-6 weeks old. You can use a heat lamp hung over the box. At that time, their true feathers have grown to keep them warm. You can discontinue using the heat lamps if it has gotten warm outside (if you purchased your chicks in the middle of the summer). If it is

cooler at night, they will still need the heat lamps. If the chicks, however, huddle under the lamps, it is a good indication that they still need them. They also require enough space to be able to get away from the lamps if they get too hot. (Yes, they will cook if it gets too hot, and they can't cool down).

The bottom of the box should be lined with wood shavings or crushed dried leaves. If the bottom of the container is slippery, they may have trouble standing.

You may need to line the bottom with wire or folded newspaper. If you use shredded newspaper, the paper tends to get caught on their feet. If you want to save money, use dried leaves. Either way, this stuff makes for great compost for the garden! If the shavings are too fine, they may not be able to distinguish between the shavings and their food. If that happens, try to remove the shavings and just put food down. Hopefully they will figure out the difference.

Care
The experts do not advise handling, as the chicks are fragile (so they say). I think the more they are handled the more they become more like pets. Remember, though they can't really be trained, as they are low on the intelligence factor. They can be fun to have around. (They

are chickens after all.)

Behaviors
The first week or so all they will do is peck around and learn to look for food. They will become more curious as they grow. They will scratch at the wood chips and push them around. They love it when the bedding is completely changed. They will be busy for hours going through the new material.

As they grow, you will notice that they will start to perch on things like the water and food container. You may want to start providing other things for them to perch on and keep them off of the food and water containers.

Their peeping noises remain the same. They grow really fast. You can almost see them grow as you watch them. You will be amazed!

Excessive peeping means that something is wrong. They are just like kids crying for something. They may be too hot or too cold, or out of food or water. Be sure to check on them often in the first few weeks. (Twice a day is often!)

Nutrition
The feed depends on the intended use and the age of the bird. The main cost of raising chickens is the cost of their feed and there are

several commercial preparations available depending on the age of the birds. Remember, inadequate nutrition can result in losing the birds themselves.

Birds can also be allowed to feed on greens and fresh grass cuttings within the fence, as long as there are no chemicals used. Fresh table scraps such as stale bread and leafy vegetables can be given, which will provide a variety to their feeds as well as keep the costs down. Make sure not to overfeed them on these scraps or feed them anything that is spoiled.

Water is most important, and a constant supply of fresh clean water is essential for healthy poultry. Water consumption will increase a lot during hot weather.

Raising rabbits inside city limits

Don't let their small size and cute reputation fool you, rabbits are a great multi-purpose addition (or beginning) to any 21st century homestead. From pets and 4-H projects to terrific sources of wool, meat and manure, backyard rabbits make a fun, easy project that fulfills a variety of needs. With minimal time, space and financial requirements, raising rabbits is a great introduction to homesteading, or, for the more established, a simple way to make a little extra money.

Like everything else when it comes to starting a project, make your decision after you know the pros and cons. If your backyard is being used for survival because you don't live in the country, then the pros may outweigh the cons.

Pros:
Rabbits are well suited for *both* country and suburban areas. Since they are not considered livestock by many governmental agencies, they are permitted where other animals are not. It is still a good idea to check with local zoning authorities to determine if rabbits are allowed before making many plans. Rabbits make very little noise, making them better for suburbia than chickens, squabs, turkeys, geese, or ducks. In fact, if odor and flies are kept to a minimum, and the cages are well hidden by vegetation (a good idea anyway to protect them from the elements) it is possible that neighbors might not even know rabbits are in the yard.

Rabbits are fairly easy to raise. The does take care of the young themselves, so no hand-raising or special equipment, such as an incubator or brooder, is needed. There is rarely a need for intensive on-the-spot care.

Butchering is fairly simple and straightforward. A skilled person can take a rabbit from the cage to the freezer in 15 minutes or less. No plucking is needed.

Since some people consider rabbits as pets, some pet sitters will take care of them if the owner desires to take a vacation, or must be away for business or family emergency. This probably would only apply to very small rabbit raisers.

Space is often not a problem because cages can be stacked. Especially when compared to larger meat animals such as cattle or hogs, rabbits are much more efficient space users.

If high production is not a goal, they can be fed kitchen scraps and forage food. There are many stories of rabbits being raised during the Depression or in third-world countries eating things people would normally discard or that can be easily gathered from the surrounding area. Some food such as elm or apple branches, or some weeds such as dandelions may already be readily available.

Rabbit meat is extremely low in cholesterol and has an exceptionally high percentage of digestible protein. It is quite low in fat as well.

Cons:
Rabbits might not be the best choice if one desires to make substantial money from sell-

ing the meat. It can be fairly difficult to find a market for rabbit meat. Individuals are permitted to process their own meat for family use, but not for anyone else. Some folks can get around this problem by selling the fryer live and butcher the animal as a free service. This can work for friends or relatives, but not for any commercial endeavor. Processors in the US are few and far between. There also might not be a "bunny runner" available to take the fryers to a processor. Even if a processor is nearby, there is no guarantee it will accept shipment from a new source.

Rabbits do not thrive in hot weather. Therefore, they are much better suited for temperate or cooler climes.

It is more expensive to produce one pound of meat from a rabbit than other small meat animals. Likewise, on a small scale, as most backyard setups are, the meat is often *more expensive* than if it were purchased in the store.

In some parts of the world, especially the United States, rabbits are not commonly considered a meat animal. Consequently, a prospective breeder needs to be selective when choosing with whom he discusses his avocation. He must be sensitive to those who view rabbits as pets. Pets are loving members of a family, and most people would never consider eating their dog or cat. Rabbits are cute and furry; so many people are repulsed at the thought of killing and eating them. This is called the "Easter Bunny Syndrome."

Getting started

First of all, before buying your initial stock, you need to think about housing. There are many plans for building your own hutches available on the Internet and in books but some things in general need to be considered.

Rabbits are prey to many other animals, so they need to be protected. Make sure you keep their cages off the ground and insure they are sturdy enough to protect the rabbits from dogs, coyotes and other threats.

Rabbits need a clean dry environment that protects them from the weather to thrive well. This means keeping them in an area that has good ventilation in warmer weather but can be closed up to keep them warm and draft free in winter. Overhead cover is essential to keep them dry and happy.

Housing

There are different approaches to housing rabbits. One is known as "colonizing the herd," where all rabbits are kept in a common area. This method is more common in Europe, where it has enjoyed some success, than North

America. Disease can easily spread and wipe out a colonized herd faster than one where the members are housed in separate cages. For these and other reasons I do not recommend this practice, and instead recommend individual cages for each breeding rabbit. Wire cages of at least six square feet in area are preferable for breeding does and weaned litters. Bucks' cages should have at least five square feet of floor space. Cage height should be about 18 inches. All cages should be cleaned on a regular basis, and those kept outside should be well protected from the weather. The use of older style all-wood hutches is discouraged because of the difficulty in thoroughly cleaning and disinfecting them. A benefit of older hutches is that they are easier on rabbits' feet, especially that of pregnant does. To help combat this problem with wire cages a small hard plastic mat may be placed on the cage floor.

Cages can either be store bought (already assembled), bought as a kit that you put together, or built entirely from scratch. It is advisable to build them entirely from wire that will last longer, but can be built with a wood frame if you have scrap wood lying around. After you have planned and built your hutches, you need to acquire the other equipment needed for this endeavor. Specifically, what you need are feeders, some way of getting water to the rabbits, feed and nest boxes.

Other Equipment

Most people use the galvanized metal self-feeders available at most feed stores and cost around $5 each. Make sure you get the ones with the fine screen on the bottom as this only cost a few cents more but require less work as the "fines" (small bits of feed) will fall through, and you won't have to clean out the feeders as often.

As far as watering goes, many people use the hanging water bottles ($5 ea). Another tip here, get the ones with the hinge top as they are much easier to fill up, the other type has to be removed from the bracket, and filled from the bottom. For only a little more money you can save a lot of extra work in the long run. Rabbits need a lot of water for their size so each one will need their own bottle, and they need to be disinfected on occasion. Another option is to install an automatic watering system, which some people do but in my opinion, unless you plan on raising a lot of rabbits, it is not really worth the time and expense to build this type of system. The one thing not to do is to use any kind of water bowls or crocks; they will soil them and turn them over every time you turn around.

Feed

Feed (pellets) can be bought at the feed stores

and are fairly inexpensive for a 50 lb. bag. I suggest that if kept in the original bag in tightly sealed containers (such as plastic garbage cans) feed will stay good at least six months so stock up as you can afford it. Good old alfalfa hay is also good to feed them. You will need to install some way of attaching the hay up off the floor with either a "hay rack" or by just tying it up with wire to keep it from falling on the floor and getting soiled. In addition, table scraps can be given to the rabbits, they love lettuce, celery, carrots etc and go crazy for a treat like apple or pear slices once in awhile. If you plan on only feeding your rabbits commercial feed, then they will get plenty of salt. However, if you plan on feeding mostly hay and scraps, you will need to get some salt spools to put in each cage.

How many rabbits to start and how old should they be?

Those just starting in rabbits need to examine their reasons for getting into the hobby and what goals one hopes to achieve. A common mistake is to start with too many rabbits. A reasonable starting point might be two bucks and two does. It is recommended that these rabbits be purchased while they are still young. This way, they will have a chance to become acclimated to their new surroundings prior to breeding. However, beware of breeders selling older animals. A valid concern would be why he or she is selling an older animal. It costs money to feed animals and it is not cost-effective for a meat breeder to keep it past the time it reaches slaughter weight. They might be culls that do not perform well. On the other hand, culls from a show breeder with meat-type goals may be satisfactory.

As the new breeder gets accustomed to the rabbit hobby, then, and *only then*, should he or she decide to increase the size of the herd, and then slowly. A common error is to grow too big too fast.

Buying rabbits
Obviously, before you can start breeding rabbits, you have to acquire some to begin with. There are several ways to go about this; first off, you have to find someone in your area that raises rabbits so that you can purchase them. Look in the papers and ask at the feed stores for someone to contact. Once contact is made, go out and visit them and tell them what you want and what you intend to do with them. Explain that you intend to raise them for food and not pets. What you are looking for is "meat" rabbits, which are medium-weight breeds like New Zealand Whites and Californians. While they may not grow as big as the "giant breeds", they grow more quickly to fryer size, which is what you want.

As I just stated, the best way to start is to buy at least two does, and two bucks insuring they are from different bloodlines, and here is why. What you can do is breed one buck with one doe, and the other buck with the other doe. Once the does from these litters mature, you can now breed the other buck with them (different bloodlines) and not have any inbreeding, which is never good for the herd. Another option is to mate one buck with both does and then breed the second buck with the does from these original litters. There are many ways of doing this with different numbers of rabbits that you start with.

Breeding

Rabbits are considered mature when they are 5 to 6 months old. I feel that a good practice is best to wait until 6 months to be safe. To check to see if a doe is ready, flip her over and look at the vulva, if it is a red or purple color, most likely she is ready. If pink then most likely she is not ready. Take the doe to be bred and put her in the buck's cage (always in his cage). It will not take long as they know automatically what to do and will take care of business quickly. If the doe resists his advances and will not submit after a few minutes, take the doe out and try again the next day, or try another buck. If everything goes well and it usually does, go ahead and put the doe back in her cage. Sometimes after mating the buck has been known to get rather mean and start biting the doe so do not leave them together unattended. A good practice is to mate the same two again about 12 hours later just to make sure. Note here, if the buck falls over or makes a shrieking sound after mating, this is normal and quite comical!

Now all you have to do is wait, gestation period is about 28 to 30 days so after about 10 days to two weeks you can check the doe if you want by flipping her over and feeling around for the babies. At this stage, they are about the size of marbles. About 3 days before they are due, it is time to put the nest box in the doe's cage. Put some clean, dry hay in it and get ready. They usually have their babies at night and a little while before birth, the doe will start arranging the hay and pulling fur off her belly to make a nest for the little ones. This fur can be saved for later if you have a doe that does not pull her fur on her own.

If everything goes well, you will have 6 to 10 bunnies in the nest box. This is a normal size litter but can be more. You need to inspect the litter and pull out any dead ones to keep her from eating them. Wear gloves to keep your scent off of the babies. You might want to give her a bit of apple to occupy her while you are looking the litter over. At birth the bunnies look like mice but this is only temporary as when they get about 10 days old their eyes will be open and they will soon start looking like small rabbits. When they first get a full coat of fur is when they are the cutest but it is important not to get attached to them or let children name them as it needs to be understood that these animals are meant as a source of food and not as pets. Easier said than done, I know! Keep the nest box clean and remove it after a few weeks. When the litter is four to five weeks old, you can rebreed the doe if you want.

After the bunnies are weaned (6 to 8 weeks) it is time to decide on what to do with them. Some of the rabbits may be kept for future breeders, and the rest butchered or fattened up a little more first, but it is important to remember that hanging on to them for longer than necessary will only mean more cost in feed. Let them nurse as long as possible as it costs you no more in feed but puts more weight on them. Furthermore, do not remove all the little ones at one time, as it is better for the doe to dry up gradually. You may put all the weaned bunnies in one cage but after a few months they all need their own,

Slaughtering and butchering

It should be understood that dispatching (selling or butchering) rabbits is *never* a pleasant task. Even after many years of processing, many, if not most breeders still dread the job.

That said, it is still a necessary chore.

To facilitate butchering, feed should be withheld from the animal for 24 hours prior to slaughter. This helps clear out the digestive system. Since rabbits practice coprophagy the intestines will still not be completely clear. For this reason, some people choose to withhold feed for 48 hours.

There are several methods that can be used to dispatch a rabbit. It is my opinion that *top consideration* should be given to methods that cause the animal the *least stress* and are *safe* for the breeder to use.

One method entails holding the back legs up and, with the dominant hand, quickly pulling the neck down while firmly tilting the head up, dislocating the skull from the spine. This method, sometimes called "twist and crunch," requires skill and is not recommended unless the person is experienced and has sufficient strength to perform it properly.

Most people hit the rabbit on the back of the head with a bat or similar object either at or just above the base of the skull. With both these techniques, the rabbit is hung by its back legs and the head removed for proper bleeding. Some people slit the throat right after hanging to bleed the animal.

A third way to slaughter a fryer is simple decapitation on a hard surface, similar to chopping a chicken's head off, prior to hanging. Drawbacks include having a bruised shoulder area on the carcass, the possibility of losing a finger or worse, and needing at least two persons to do the act. Lastly, recently it has been found that this method is not the most humane because the brain continues to be aware for several seconds after severing.

There is another choice called the "broomstick method." With this method, the rabbit is placed on a firm surface, preferably the ground. A treat may be given to the rabbit. A sturdy broomstick is laid across the rabbit's neck while positioning its front legs pointing towards the back of the rabbit. The dispatcher then steps on the broomstick on either side of the rabbit and quickly grasps the hind legs and firmly pulls them straight upward. The person should pull until he feels the neck break. Two simple clues indicate that the rabbit is indeed dead — one is that the head easily swings back and forth; the other is bleeding through the nose, ears, or mouth. A definite plus to this method is that it can be done by only one person and avoids the possible difficulties encountered with a swinging axe. A drawback is that it, too, can produce a bruised shoulder area.

Once hung the front feet may be cut off with

small pruning shears. Spraying the carcass with water helps keep loose fur down. A knife is used to cut around the back legs below the hocks. A cut is then made along the inside of the back legs from one foot to the other. After cutting through the base of the tail the skin may be peeled off like a sweater. A slit is then made down the front from near the anus to the sternum along a visible "seam." Special care should be taken not to nick the bladder in the process. The entrails are removed; the kidneys and liver saved if desired. The sternum is cut and lungs, heart, and trachea removed. The heart may also be saved. Lastly, the pubic bone is cut, and rectum removed.

After the carcass is rinsed of stray fur and blood it is then dropped in a bucket of ice water. After about five minutes it can be placed in another bucket of ice water. Some people prefer three. Each subsequent bucket cools the meat further, completing the bleeding process and making it easier to cut into pieces. Lastly, the carcass is cut up as desired, usually into seven to nine pieces, placed in a "Ziplock" freezer bag, and into the freezer. A fryer rabbit may be placed in one gallon- or two pint-sized freezer bags.

County extension offices may have copies of publications that explain butchering in greater detail, and with photographs.

Raising miniature goats

Some folks may cringe at the idea of caring for a goat in your own backyard. Truth be told, it is not complicated or risky. The important thing is to recognize the pros and cons of keeping goats, especially caring for them as food producers or even pets.

As long as you know how to keep them and know the basic principle of caring for goats, it won't lay a health or hygienic risk to the residential district.

Alas, many are not aware there are 100's of different goat breeds and every, if not all, are domesticated either for their milk, meat or pelt. They are virtually innocuous and do not pose any kind of lethal menace to human race.

The only kind of menace these goats could make with the locals in communities is the possible headache locals could have from the continuous bleating when the goats need to be fed. Besides that, these animals are timid and serene beasts. But generally, goats are not dangerous.

Here are a couple ideas to check into if you wish to practice raising goats in your own backyard.

Raising miniature goats

As I just stated, there are 100s of different goat breeds but living in the city or suburbia, where land is scarce, I suggest you investigate the smaller goat breeds. There are small goat breads for both milk and meat production that are smaller than most large dogs. I mentioned in chapter 4 three types of goats. One of those mentioned was a miniature goat bred for their milk production.

Miniature breeds of goats that are hardy, friendly, and utterly adorable are the **Nigerian dwarf goats**. Their friendly dispositions and compact size make them perfect for large back yards, small farms, 4H, and as pets. Goats get very lonely if raised alone, so it is suggested you have at least two for your backyard livestock.

Dwarf goats are still livestock animals and need plenty of outdoor space and room to play. However, they don't need as much as their larger cousins.

Fencing

Make sure to make a fence around your goat shed, putting it up to an adequate height, enough to keep your critters from making their way out of their shelter or grazing field. Fence a 20-by-20-foot area with fencing that is four to five feet tall for one or two goats. Goats are intelligent and can escape easily, so inspect your fence regularly for holes or breakage.

Housing

Provide housing for your miniature goats. An 8-by-10-foot shed or doghouse is appropriate for one or two goats. Miniature goats don't like to get wet so some sort of shelter from the elements is a must. Because your goats are very small, you don't have to build them a barn, unless you already have one on your property.

Feeding

Twice a day, feed your little goats a good quality hay, like alfalfa or red clover. Place the hay onto a hayrack above the ground, as miniature goats are not likely to eat food from the ground. This also protects against intestinal worms.

Males are prone to developing kidney/urinary tract stones (calculi) so should be maintained on a low protein, low calcium diet. A mineral balance achieved with a goat-formula mineral supplement aids in the prevention of urinary calculi. I recommend feeding males limited grain once they are over six months to one year of age, augmented with a goat-formulated mineral supplement. Avoiding high-protein feed supplements significantly reduces the risk of developing urinary calculi (blockage). You can give your wether or buck a veggie or fruit treat while the girls get their grain. If you insist on feeding grain to (mature) males, use a "Lamb Finisher" pellet. These contain a urine acidifier, ammonium chloride, which helps prevent calculi and is the grain of choice; not more than 1/8 - 1/4 cup per day. If you've had a problem with UC, you might try adding extra urine acidifiers.

Does benefit from alfalfa and/or increased grain -16 or 18% protein goat feed (ex. Caprine Challenger by Blue Seal) when pregnant or lactating. Mature, non-breeding animals may be maintained on good-quality hay alone. Kids are growing and benefit from a high-protein diet. I strongly recommend feeding kids a starter pellet medicated with a coccidia stat for their first six months. It is also a good idea to have your vet check the stool for coccidia and other parasites regularly when your goats are young and annually when mature.

Special Care
Provide a Tetanus C and D shot once a year, and a BoSe shot every six months. Consult a veterinarian, as your goats may need additional care or shots depending on the area where they live or if pregnant. De-worm your goats. Goats are susceptible to different parasites in various regions of the country. The best way to know what parasites your goats need to be treated for is to take a stool sample periodi-

cally to a veterinarian for testing. De-worm the goats according to your veterinarian's directions.

Trim your miniature goat's hooves and groom it regularly to prevent problems. Hooves must be trimmed as needed: the bottom should be flat without edges curling under. Scissor type garden pruning shears work well.

Put goat "toys" in your pasture or pen. Goats are intelligent and playful animals. Providing them with toys will prevent boredom. Stumps and logs as well as large cable spools will provide goats with a place to jump, climb, and play. Provide a small rock pile for climbing and to help wear down the goats' hoofs.

Health
All goats need immunizations to stay healthy. I recommend you give all goats their Bar-Vac CDT(clostridium perfringens types C&D tetanus toxoid) first immunizations as a kid. When the goat reaches one-year-old, and every year after, it should receive a booster Bar-Vac CDT injection.

Goats do get parasites, (worms, lice, fleas, ticks) and goats need to be de-wormed 4x yearly. Alternate wormers for goats because they can & will build a resistance to wormers. Worm according to seasons: Ivomec Plus wormer orally in spring & fall (kills lice and other external parasites also). Safeguard paste (@ 5x the dosage) in winter & summer. This keeps goats worm & parasite free all year.

Make sure that goats have a trace mineral salt (it will be the red kind) at all times. Goats will need these minerals that are missing in the environment to keep them healthy. And always keep common baking soda available for your goats. A goat eats baking soda to keep urine acidity in the proper range, and it helps with digestion. Goats will self medicate. They know when they need the soda and how much they need. A goat can lap up an average of two tablespoons of baking soda per day.

Never overfeed your goat oats because it will bloat. Bloat is an excessive accumulation of gas trapped in numerous tiny bubbles, making it impossible for the goat to burp. If this should ever happen, a cup of oil (corn, peanut, or mineral) or baking soda will usually relieve the condition. However, be careful giving any goat an oily substance orally. It can choke because the oil consistency is different than most liquids. Bloat can be fatal, another good reason to keep baking soda available.

Breeding Nigerian dairy goats
Before I go into breeding, I suggest that you don't raise bucks for breeding while raising

them in the city or suburban areas. Find a good farm that will breed your does so you don't have to have the buck on limited property space. The bucks should have their own pen to keep them away from the does until you are ready to breed them. So with that said, Nigerian goats breed year round. Many owners have their does impregnated three times in two years, giving the doe at least a 6-month break. Of course, this is a personal choice for each breeder. The gestation period for a doe is 145 to 153 days. For the most part, Nigerian goats are a hearty breed with few kidding problems. New babies average about 2 pounds at birth but grow quickly. Watch out for those little bucks! Bucklings can be fertile as young as seven weeks of age. Make sure you wean does and bucks separately to help you avoid unintentional breeding.

Does can be bred at 7-8 months of age if they have reached a mature size. Some breeders prefer to wait until they are at least one year or older. Nigerian goat does can have several kids at a time, 3 and 4 being common with some quintuplet births occurring. Nigerian goats are generally good mothers, able to take care of their babies should you leave them to do the raising of the kids. They can also provide a surprising amount of milk for their size if you decide you want your own delicious goat milk or cheese.

Bucks can be used for service as young as three months of age and easily by the time they are 7 or 8 months old. Nigerian goat bucks are vigorous breeders and are gentle enough to be used for hand breeding (contained) or pasture breeding where one buck is available for several does as they come into estrus. Both methods are used successfully.

Small fruit trees

An important thing to remember about raising goats is they will eat just about anything. If you let your goats run free in your back yard, even though they are small, they will eat all your potted vegetables, and branches off your dwarf fruit trees as far as they can get.

Speaking of fruit trees, which is an important subject when thinking how to survive in the city or suburban homestead setting, we will discuss them next.

Plant dwarf fruit trees

With a little creativity, even gardeners with small yards can enjoy the homegrown fresh fruit. Dwarf fruit trees are easily incorporated into ornamental landscaping, assuming the location otherwise fills the bill, and there are several other viable space-saving planting strategies. Not only do dwarf and semi-dwarf trees take up less space than standard varieties, they also bear fruit sooner and are more easily pruned and cared for. Choose varieties that do well in your soil and climate conditions, and be sure to provide cross-pollinators if needed. Water and fertilize trees consistently with their type, and prune for good form and productivity.

Container plantings
The most creative spacing possible for dwarf fruit trees is to take up no garden space at all — planting trees instead in containers kept on sunny, south-facing, wind-protected decks or patios. According to Four Winds Growers, gardeners can bring potted fruit trees indoors for freeze protection. Grow trees in plastic containers so pots are movable, and make sure they have adequate drain holes. Use light, well-drained planting mix without added fertilizers or wetting agents; make sure pots don't sit in standing drainage water. Keep tree roots cooler and improve aesthetics by "nesting" plain planting pots inside larger, more decorative pots.

Multi-tree plantings
Save space with dwarf fruit trees by planting multiple trees together — you read that right — preferably combining several compatible cultivars/pollinators together. With this technique, you can grow two, three, or four trees

in the space of one. Space tree trunks just 24 inches apart, and tip trees slightly outward from the center. Finish each multiple planting by pruning away any center branches that would otherwise cross.

Tiered plantings

However creatively you plant them, keep in mind that fruit trees need good air drainage as much as well-drained soil. Cold air flows down hill just as water does, and fruit trees in low-lying areas will freeze before trees up-slope do. So, another way to grow trees in a limited space is to create vertical planting beds, or tiers, in some otherwise unused, or unusable, space, providing better air drainage and freeze protection in the process. Planting dwarf or semi-dwarf fruit trees in sunny stepped-up, or tiered, raised beds can make good productive use of a steep hill or rocky waste.

Pollinating your plants

Fruit trees, vegetable plants and all flowering plants need to be pollinated. If you live in the city, you may not want to have a beehive. Depending on how close together your neighbor is, you may not get enough airflow to do the job. So what is a city homesteader to do? God created the Mason Bees.

What are Mason Bees?

Orchard Mason bees are native North American bees. They live all across the United States and Southern Canada, but are particularly common in the Pacific Northwest, especially in the Puget Sound area and western Cascade Mountains. They are also called "blue orchard bees" and scientists know them as Osmia lignaria. They are beautiful insects, about 1/3 inch long and blue black with a metallic sheen. Unfortunately, they are sometimes mistaken for large flies (look closely - they have two pairs of wings and are not interested in garbage!). The females are somewhat larger than the males, and the males have a white hairy face. Like all bees, Mason bees collect flower pollen as a protein source for their young and get their energy from flower nectar. In shopping for groceries, they carry pollen from flower to flower, achieving pollination.

A number of things set Mason bees apart from other bees:

- **Solitary:** Each female bee builds a nest by herself, lays eggs, seals the nest, and goes about her business. She receives no help from other bees, so there is no colony or "hive" as in honeybees or bumblebees.
- **Live together:** Mason bees are attracted to each other. They like to build their nests in aggregations.
- **Safe:** As with other solitary bees, Mason bees are gentle and shy. They have a

stinger (actually it is an egg guide), but they use it only when they are in serious danger, as when they are purposely caught in the hand. They do not attack to defend their nest or arouse each other in alarm.

- **Specialized pollinators:** Mason bees prefer to forage on flowers in the apple family, including many varieties of apples, cherries, plums, peaches, and similar "stone fruits." Because they specialize on these plants, they are exceptionally good pollinators of them. They will forage on other flowers as well.

- **Hard working:** Orchard Mason bees are adapted to a cool climate and can fly in chilly, even drizzly weather. Thus, they are often busy pollinating when honeybees remain inside the hive.

- **Build with bricks:** Like the wisest little pig, Orchard Mason bees build their nests with bricks (sort of). Each egg chamber in the nest is sealed with a partition of ordinary mud. The entire nest is also sealed with a hardened mud capping. This is why they are called "mason" bees.

The above features make Orchard Mason bees the perfect pollinator for those who have a small number of fruit trees, but may not want to manage honeybee hives. They are also a fascinating wild creature that can be easily encouraged to colonize the backyard garden environment to the benefit of the gardener, homeowner, and nature lover. Mason bees are totally safe, even around children and pets.

There are Internet web sites that sell and ship these amazing bees. You can also find places that sell already made Mason bee hives. I suggest you look at plan designs and build your own. They are simple to build and very low cost with materials from any home building or craft store.

The small homestead farmer can do many of the ideas brought up in this chapter on either city or suburban homesteading sites. The same holds true for the apartment farmer using patios, if available. So don't let the size of the land or where you live stop you from starting to live healthy and providing for yourself.

Chapter 6

Can we survive alone or

do we need others?

Up to this point in this book, I have shown you it is possible to survive in the full homesteading mode if it becomes necessary. The whole purpose of this book is to learn to cultivate a life style for better health and to build self-reliance in your ability to survive off the land when necessary.

If we live according to God's plan we could own a "Wee Bit Of Heaven." Even the Bible shows what happens when those of like minds gather together for the good of all involved.

"All the believers were together and had everything in common. They sold property and possessions to give to anyone who had need. Every day they continued to meet together in the temple courts. They broke bread in their homes and ate together with glad and sincere hearts, praising God and enjoying the favor of all the people. And the Lord added to their number daily those who were being saved." Acts 2: 44-47 (NIV)

A community of like believers
Now I know what happened in the Bible time period was for the survival of Christians who were being persecuted by the Jews, but survival is still survival no matter what may have caused it.

In the time when wagon trains headed west to find a place to build a home and work off the land, one of the things that sprang up was a small town where people could come together to trade their goods for necessities they didn't produce themselves. Most homesteaders did not produce everything, but if they had something someone else had an abundance of, they would trade, or as we call it today, barter with others for things they needed. In order to do this, people with like minds and desires needed to work together for the common good of everyone.

This philosophy still holds true today. We can see this attitude practiced among the Amish people. Not only do they live in the same general areas but are there for one another when someone is in trouble. The Amish people are a very tight group because they believe in what their lifestyle represents. They can be found in many communities at farmer's markets and along country road stands selling their products.

In Fulton, NY, where I was born and lived many years of my life, there existed in different parts of the town, small clusters of various ethnic families who spoke their common languages. They had many things in common which held them together. They stuck very close and practiced many of their customs. This sometimes led to some factions between these groups but in general, at least where we lived, we all got along together with our differences.

Connecting with others

This philosophy will also help modern-day homesteading. You might want to find homesteaders in your area because you don't want to feel like an odd duck. After all, your parents, relatives, and friends may be terrified at the prospect of you living alone on that piece of land. When you start talking about how much fun goats are, your friends begin to stare at you like you've just sprouted a second head.

What's a poor homesteader to do?

Actually, there are ways to find others who share your homesteading zeal. Here are some tips to get you on the road to friendships with other like-minded self-reliant folks.

Start an online Yahoo group

Thanks to our modern-day technology, you can live in an isolated area and not be isolated. Look for a local online homesteading Yahoo group, and if you don't find one, start one. Post your own comments regularly about your homesteading passion. If *you* were looking for a Yahoo online group that focuses on homesteading in your locale, chances are someone else will be as well. This practice is only good as long as we still have the Internet and not already in a meltdown.

Go to the library

Librarians tend to have a great wealth of information anyway, but the librarian of a small rural town might help you find and create homesteading communities by giving you names of those who own goats or cows, make and sell cheese, or sell hay and vegetables in the summertime. Such activities are the sign of a homestead addiction. Visit the library in person, and you may be able to leave fliers advertising your new local online group (see above).

Your local 4-H group

If you have children, this is a great way to get to know others in your area that are as passionate about self-sufficient living as you are. And your kids will have fun too. Most everyone who joins the 4-H group at schools that still have them are usually country dwellers.

Local Home schooling groups

Homesteading and home schooling tend to go hand in hand. Become self-reliant about growing your own food, and you'll soon become self-reliant-minded about how you want your children educated. Go online and find your state home school association (virtually every state now has one). Look up online groups and contact them to help you find homesteaders and homesteading communities. They are bound to know one or two self-reliant people in your area.

Your farmers' supply or feed store

Homesteaders tend to have critters, and that means they'll be frequenting these places regularly, so these are excellent places to locate homesteading communities. Ask the manager if he knows of anyone you can contact, and while you're at it, ask him if he has a bulletin board where you can post one of your flyers.

Attend auctions

You can find these by doing an online search by typing in the name of your state along with the phrase "livestock auctions." Your local newspaper or Penny Saver Magazine will often advertise local auctions. Find an auction that is close by and spend a morning there. You'll not only get the chance to locate homesteading communities, but you'll also learn a lot of useful information about livestock.

Join a national online homestead forum
A great one to help you locate local homesteading communities is **Country Life and Homesteading**. Join it and then ask if there are any other members from your area.

Strength in numbers

Homesteaders (hundreds of years ago) often banded together and traveled for miles to help their neighbors for things such as barn raisings, home raisings, quilting bees, etc. They would help each other with plowing, planting, and harvesting crops and hay. This was not the only reason for banning together. They also banded together for protection. This gave them a sense of "community" regardless of how far apart they were in actual miles. It's a way of life, a state of mind, a method of thinking that requires a return to a simpler time when trusting your neighbors was the norm rather than the exception. It's also about being independent and self-sufficient but willing to lend a hand (or accept one) when it's needed. Every town & city in this country started out in the beginning as a few people, a community of folks who banded together & worked together for protection & survival.

Preparedness and self-sufficiency were a normal everyday way of life 150 years ago. They had to buy in large quantities, because they might not get to town for another six months or a year. They had to learn to put up their own food, raise & hunt for their meat supply, and take care of themselves. Learning to be that prepared and self-sufficient takes some doing, but it can be done. Old skills are dying out in many places, but they're good to learn on a homestead. Conveniences are nice to have, but it's nice to know you could do without them if you had to.

The things that made coming together as a community then are still true today for the modern homesteader. There becomes strength in numbers. Those individuals who don't heed the signs of possible impending need to become a survivor and self-reliant, may become your enemy and want all you have worked hard for.

Looking out for one another

If the community that you have put together for the benefits reported above is one that is very close in proximity to one another, then you all need to start to have conversations on what you all will do as a group if there is a world melt down economically. You and your family, along with the community you belong to of homesteaders are able to take care of yourselves, but the majority of the world will not be. There is no way that your little farm and those of your friends can take care of world hunger. In order for your survival, you need to have a plan of action to protect yourselves.

There is something to be said for getting to know your neighbors, interacting with them, learning their political and religious leanings, and having non-traditional conversations that center, in one way or another, on personal, neighborhood and community defense.

Organize neighbour-hood watch groups
When you go away, stop delivery of your mail or newspapers or ask a neighbor to pick them up. Create the illusion that someone is home and following everyday routines.

The bottom line in all of this is, use common sense. You will reduce your chances of becoming a crime victim, and it won't cost you a thing. Furthermore, be a good neighbor. Keep an eye on your neighbors' homes, livestock and equipment. If you see any suspicious persons or activity, report it to the Sheriff's Office.

Because phone systems may not be working,

a means of warning each other needs to be implemented. CB radios, short-wave, or even walkie-talkies can be used. If we do experience an economic collapse, hyperinflation or any scenario that leads to a breakdown in the rule of law in the United States, we can fully expect gangs to make their way across the country side looting, pillaging and killing any who stand in their way. Like the rest of society, they will be struggling to obtain valuable resources like food and gas. They will be heavily armed. They will be using military tactics, and they will have absolutely no qualms about killing you and your family – not just to acquire your food and supplies – but for fun.

As much as I will be willing to help some in need in order to survive, I don't feel God want us to let heavily armed gangs just come onto our homestead to rape, kill and steal all that we have worked for our own survival without putting up a fight.

It is for this reason that, whether you do it now or after "*it*" hits the fan, building a strong community defense plan, guard rotation, and engaging in muster exercises will be absolutely critical to your survival.

If we're talking about the "worst case," understand that "worst case" means contemplating extreme scenarios that will require you and those around you to take lethal, sometimes brutal, measures to defend self and home.

Using the barter system

Barter is a method of exchange by which goods or services are directly exchanged for other goods or services without using a medium of exchange, such as money. It is usually bilateral, but may be multilateral, and often exists parallel to monetary systems in most developed countries, though to a very limited extent. Barter usually replaces money as the method of exchange in times of monetary crisis, such as when the currency may be either unstable (e.g., hyperinflation or deflationary spiral) or simply unavailable for conducting commerce.

Tax implications
In the United States, the sales a barter exchange makes are considered taxable revenue by the IRS, and the gross amount of a barter exchange member's sales are reported to the IRS by the barter exchange via a 1099-B form. The requirement for barter exchanges to report members sales was enacted in the Tax Equity and Fiscal Responsibility Act of 1982. According to the IRS, "The fair market value of goods and services exchanged must be included in the income of both parties."

Other countries do not have the reporting requirement that the U.S. does concerning the proceeds from barter transactions, but taxation is handled the same way as a cash transaction. If one barters for a profit, one pays the appropriate tax; if one generates a loss in the transaction, they have a loss. Bartering for business is also taxed accordingly as business income or business expense. Many barter exchanges require that one register as a business.

Items to barter
Now that I have gotten possible tax implications out of the way, so no one can accuse me of not warning you, let's look at what we may have to barter with when we have a global collapse and we need not worry about the IRS.

The fiat money is fizzling out to nothing more than ashes, and is worth less than the paper it is printed on. When it finally happens, people will be in a bad way. We live in a society where money is nothing more than a symbol of control. No money means no food, supplies, medical care or services. However, does an economic collapse really mean the end of having the means to acquire the basics needs to have a good life? No it does not. Not by a long shot.

Money has not always been this paper and coin device of control for the gain of greedy Elitists.

There was a time not too long ago where people across the Globe traded for goods. The Bartering System, in my opinion, cannot be beat when it comes to a truly smooth flowing economy. Who in their right mind would want paper money when it is worthless? No one will, but everyone who is on the right track will want things like vegetable/fruit seeds, homeopathic medicines, hygiene/medical supplies, metals and more, which of course are items that can be used to survive and dare I say it, live well without money.

The Barter System is simple, and the rules are obvious. First of all, if it is to work well, then the initial requirements are Common Sense, no Greed, no Ego, Co-Existence without war and hopefully crime at a minimum, decency and of course goods to trade. Now combine all of that and set up a Barter market that is the combination of a Swap Meet, Farmers Market, and something similar to the Penny Saver magazine. All that is needed are people to come with items to barter with the Trade Good Suppliers and, if done correctly, people will return home with the items they were in need of. It is really that simple?

Well, it is that simple to me, but then again, I am painting this picture for you in a scenario where all participants work together in the bartering system. What is great about this system is that there is no exact set value rate on a particular item. It all depends on the participants trading. Someone may barter onion seeds and a few working batteries for a chicken while another receives a small first-aid kit for trading a shovel. There are towns beginning to use this system in the U.S. currently. Endless possibilities mean a greater chance of finding what you need at a barter market.

Now let's talk about what can be used for bartering and what items will be in serious demand in the event of an "Economic Collapse." Many will tell you to store up on gold and silver because it will become the new currency. I don't necessarily have a problem with that statement but realistically most people now cannot even afford to purchase them. However, consider using these metals as well as others such as copper and tin as an item to use for Bartering. If at all possible, I recommend avoiding that Cash for Gold businesses and keeping your jewelry so you could use it for trading. One gold or silver necklace could be segmented into smaller pieces and used for trade. Other items to consider are seeds, medical supplies, sugar, coffee and batteries to name just a few. Don't limit yourself to just those items because you may be surprised what you have already that can be used.

So as you can see this barter system concept

really is not that hard and can be done quite easily if you plan correctly as best as you are able. When you get a chance spend some time going through everything you possess and just take an inventory. Perhaps even stockpile a few items you already own...you know....just in case of an emergency. You might just feel a little better after doing so. Being proactive in your own preparation for an emergency WILL give you some peace and reassurance, I guarantee.

A world without the fiat currency control is a better world for us all and life using a barter system is a system that can be used to not just survive, but to live a fruitful life. If we are to continue as a co-existing human race, then we are going to have to go back to the basics. It is not an option but is a reality we must face and accept freely.

Chapter 7

Where does God or religion

fit into this picture?

Design by Robert Frost

I found a dimpled spider, fat and white,
On a white heal-all, holding up a moth
Like a white piece of rigid satin cloth—
Assorted characters of death and blight
Mixed ready to begin the morning right,
Like the ingredients of a witches' broth—
A snow-drop spider, a flower like a froth,
And dead wings carried like a paper kite.

What had that flower to do with being white,
The wayside blue and innocent heal-all?
What brought the kindred spider to that
height,
Then steered the white moth thither in the
night?
What but design of darkness to appall?—
If design govern in a thing so small.

God the creator of all things, the power and essence that makes it all happen and is in all things here on Earth, cannot be ignored when we consider our ability to survive. The things that we do to our environment and the bounty we receive from it is a well-balanced plan created by God.

Glenn Kimball, before he died in 2010, had a web site (ancientmanuscripts.org) where he sent out many informative emails to all on his list. I would like to share a part of one that has inspired me very much.

NOW YOU SEE IT AND NOW YOU DON'T
Glenn Kimball
December 1, 2008

There is so much of what is real that we can't access with our five senses. Of a very large electromagnetic band of wavelengths, we see an infinitesimal part. The same is true for the rest of the five senses. We can't see radio and television waves. We can't see gravity or magnetic fields. We can't directly see emotions, thoughts, culture, history or memory. However, each of these things affects us in the real world. One has to wonder how many things pass us without notice every second of every day. If we could see just the telephone calls that circulate around us, we would be amazed. Science has to ask itself the question, "what don't they see?" Is it possible that deity or aliens or some other aberrational life form could walk right passed us unnoticed? Are these life forces capable of masking their presence? Do they need to be masked by their very nature? Do they walk passed us in a dimension that is all around us, but isn't accessible to the eye? The answer has to be that not only is it possible that this happens; it is likely that this happens.

With all the traffic going on around us all the time unnoticed, there has to be some sort of a cosmic set of traffic laws. Perhaps that is exactly what deity was trying to explain to Adam and Eve in the Garden of Eden. The universe does have a cosmic set of traffic laws that operate like a prime directive mandate. Those who violate that set of cosmic traffic laws pay the consequences. The organization of the universe contains the fingerprints of the cosmic set of traffic laws. The universe may appear random to a small mind, but our universe is balanced so carefully in a pattern that to deviate from what we see by one percent would spell the end of the universe as we know it. Science is just now suggesting that if the Big Bang were to have occurred just a percent or two differently the universe would not have survived. We alter the temperature of the earth five degrees, and it would kill 95% of all life. If we had twenty percent less water or oxygen, none of us would be here. If the earth weren't spinning as fast as it is we would cook or freeze. If the orbit of the planet were one percent different we would have spiraled out into space millions of years ago. If human beings doubled their life expectancy, we would have long ago ruined the planet. Between what we can't see, and the balance we can see, the earth appears like a juggler's sideshow. That is no accident. With each improbability, the odds of survival are exponentially reduced.   We are forced to conclude that there is most certainly a master juggler. The master juggler is adamant about not having interference from us.

Glenn refers to God as the master juggler. I like to refer to God as the creator and sustainer of all things and will be there to help us through all our trials and tribulations, and there will be many, when we try to survive without all the conveyance we now enjoy.

Mind, body, and spirit

Proverbs 16:24
Gracious words are a honeycomb, sweet to the soul and **healing** to the bones.

There are other ways of keeping the body healthy without doctors and medicines, and that is when we look at our body from the inside (the soul) that came from God. The soul is the core of our essence. The mind, body, and spirit must be kept in sync with each other.

Let's take Proverbs 16:24 apart for a moment. First *Gracious words* are just what they sound like. Let's start with prayer. Prayers come in many forms, but basically, it is talking to God and thanking Him in advance for the healing you expect Him to give. If you have to ask, then there may have doubt in your mind that He may say no. When you pray, indicate to God that He knows what ailments you are seeking healing for and say thank you for your healing hand upon me. When you are hungry, know that God can provide.

Luke 12:24
Consider the ravens: They do not sow or reap, they have no storeroom or barn; yet God feeds them. And how much more valuable you are than **birds**!

God will care for your safety and well being, just as He does for His other creatures.

Matthew 10:29-30
Are not two sparrows sold for a penny? Yet not one of them will fall to the ground outside your Father's care. And even the very hairs of your head are all numbered.

You have to know and trust that God has your best interest at hand. So when we pray, sing songs of praise, meditate, or just have conversations with God, He is listening and cares for your every need. I said need not wants.

Daily meditation and prayer
In the first book, I wrote and published; I indicated how I often spend time speaking with God real early in the morning while I am still

in bed. It is very quiet, and my mind is not distracted by outside distractions. It is so quiet and peaceful you can often hear your own heart beat. It is at this time I often talk to God. If you are sleeping with your spouse and don't want to wake him/her, I suggest speaking with Him with silent thoughts. If you are alone, try speaking out loud, but when you are done talking, be quiet and listen for God to speak to you through your soul.

I know, I said soul speak to you, and that is where you will hear him come through to your brain. At first, you may think you are talking to yourself, but you're not. Jesus went off to the garden to be alone and speak with God. There are only a couple of times where it is recorded that people heard God's voice out loud. While Jesus was near dead hanging on the cross, he said, "My God, my God, why have you **forsaken me**?" (Mark 15:34) There was no indication that God answered him out loud, but I am sure he did in Jesus' soul and Jesus knew what He said before he died.

Then, there was a time before his death, Jesus went with his disciples to a place called Gethsemane, and he said to them, "Sit here while I go over there and pray." He took Peter and the two sons of Zebedee along with him, and he began to be sorrowful and troubled. Then he said to them, **"My soul is over-**

whelmed with sorrow to the point of death. Stay here and keep watch with me." Going on a little farther, he fell with his face to the ground and prayed, "My Father, if it is possible, may this cup be taken from me. Yet not as I will, but as you will." (Matthew 26:36-39)

Jesus felt that his soul was troubled with his impending death. He asked his Father (God) in prayer if there may be some other way? Did God answer him? I believe so, to Jesus' soul that was troubled, and Jesus knew God's answer to the question.

I bring all this up to help you know that we too can talk with God and receive His answer to our questions. Just be quiet and listen. Your mind will know God's words and answers. The same holds true for spiritual healing. Spiritual healing is a Divine method used by many, though somewhat different, other than laying on of hands by your pastor.

What is spiritual healing?

The healing process of awakening the soul by seeking God within is a 9-step process. Spiritual healing uses Divine energy to create a path of inner healing, bringing the body, mind, and spirit into harmony with your work in the world. The time is upon us to utilize this Divine energy that is here to help us awaken into a lighter, openhearted way of living where we can all live as one in harmony with the earth and each other.

Renewed interest in spiritual healing methods will only help to further the state of modern medicine as we benefit from the experiences and knowledge of our predecessors in this noble field of healing. Unfortunately, this topic has too often been ignored and dismissed by many contemporary physicians, although these remedies have been practiced successfully for thousands of years.

The science of spiritual healing
The spiritual healing process rejuvenates the body's life force and strengthens it through several focal points throughout the body. The spiritual technique produces a neuro-psychological effect that leads the central nervous system to produce a carefully orchestrated endocrine response that relieves pain, heals the disease of the affected areas, and balances the entire body.

Now, there is a new awakening that patients who participate in their healing succeed while those who take their fate 'lying down' fail. We have been taught that when we are ill, it is the medicine that cures. Modern medicine has long ignored the self-healing ability of our body. We take healing for granted. We never realize that our body heals by itself.

Let me suggest a list of some active steps you can take to heal your mind, your soul and lastly, your body.

1) The healing power of the body is within us. There is a physician within us, and this power heals us absolutely.

2) Many of us are ignorant or are unaware of our own body's healing potential.

3) Many of us block ourselves off from this potential, preferring to trust others whom we think can 'cure' us rather than trust our own 'Infinite Intelligence' within.

4) Many of us create unhealthy circumstances with negative and self-denying thoughts, and these eventually make us sick. We fail to recognize that these are the root causes of our many illnesses.

5) We are unaware that from the day we are born, we have been bombarded with negative suggestions. Negativity begets illness.

6) Think positively; as you think, so you become! Cultivate positive attitudes of love, joy, happiness, sharing, caring, promotion of self-esteem and self-confidence.

7) Free yourself of negative thoughts. Many negative thoughts are ingrained into our subconscious mind, and they become

part of us. You and I have similar problems. And more often than not, we do
not even know that these negative
thoughts ever exist or are causing us all
these problems. We are the products of
our environment and experiences of our
lives. To be able to free ourselves from
these negative thoughts we must, first,
be aware and recognize that these negative thoughts are in us. If we keep deny-
ing that they are non-existent, there will
be no reason for change.

8) Be the active participant in your healing. You cannot remain neutral in your
healing. You can either be passive or active. The golden rule of psychosomatic
medicine is that patients must actively
take charge of their illness. Get rid of
the psychological or emotional disease
in you. Doctors cannot help you with
emotional illness. Indeed, no one can
help you deal with that, except yourself.
On the other hand, if you decide to be
passive, then by default, you are encouraging the disease to take over you. So,
the choice is yours. Again, remember
that a positive mindset promotes healing.

9) Accept the diagnosis, NOT the prognosis. When diagnosed with a serious illness, it seems the most popular question asked of the doctor is: "How much

longer do I have?" Patients then get answers like: "At most three to six months," or "Go home and get your papers in order." If we understand voodoo, then know that such answers are indeed a voodoo curse. They are like hypnotic instructions. The patients' mind will bring that prognosis to pass. Doctors give the death sentence, and the patients keep the bone pointing at themselves. Norman Cousins (Head First: The Biology of Hope) advised: "Don't deny the diagnosis, just defy the verdict that is supposed to accompany it." In short, accept the diagnosis but do not believe the prognosis. Know that the prerogative of living and dying rests with the Almighty God, not men.

Active involvement in healing
My sister Susie was found to have a stage 4 cancer in her lungs in July of 2011. This surprise revelation came unexpectedly to her and everyone who knows her because Susie was a picture of health at the time. She was teaching an aerobics workout class, writing health articles for her community newsletter, and riding her bike many miles each day.

The reason I am telling you this, is, Susie and her husband Bill, decided to take a proactive approach to her illness rather than do nothing and wait for it to all end. Following are a few emails detailing what I am referring to. This type of an approach of being positive and involved in her treatments, both medically and holistically will help her win this battle and not give up hope.

Emails written by Bill & Susie to family and friends

Date: Sunday, July 31, 2011 1:29 PM

On July 20th Sue was diagnosed with pulmonary adenocarcinoma, a rather common form of lung cancer that attacks non-smokers. Her condition is inoperable, and it is in stage 4. We presently have our primary doctor, pulmonologist and oncologist treating her. She has received extensive testing and screening to this point. Yesterday, she received a pet scan (positron emission tomography) to determine if the cancer cells have spread to other parts of the body.   We should have those results by Wednesday. There is some good news, however. Sue had to have a more current blood test done before a brain MRI was to be performed. The most current blood test showed "normal".....what that means we're not sure. The MRI was done the very next day after the blood test, and that came out clear. In the meantime, we are in the process of obtaining a 2nd opinion. It is our desire to go to the City of Hope cancer center located in Duarte, Ca. about an hr. and half driving time. The center is ranked one of the highest in the U.S.

We have a long battle ahead of us in uncharted waters. The only treatment for her condition is chemo, and that will start soon...looking at 4 months of every 3-week treatments. Sue is calm, strong and is showing an incredible display of courage. Our approach is proactive, and we are prepared to be aggressive if need be, with our insurance carrier.

Date: Tuesday, August 9, 2011 12:41 PM

Yesterday, we had our second appointment with Sue's oncologist. The PET scan revealed cancer cells in the right humerus (shoulder) and lower back (spine). The good news is that there was no evidence of any cancer cells in her other vital organs.. Sue has started prep treatment for her chemo sessions, which should start later this week. We forwarded all of Sue's test results to our doctor of 35 years in Syracuse, NY, and he concurs that chemo is the treatment we should pursue. He also has strongly recommended a mega dose of Vitamin C and Vitamin B12, 5 times a day. Sue has also increased her Omega 3 Fish oil to 9 per day and has been taking for a few weeks CoQ10 pharmaceutical grade and has been on, again, for about 2 weeks a vegetarian diet and lots of Sencha green tea.

Our request for a second opinion was denied on the basis that the same care is available in our medical group. We are not buying that! It's our opinion that their conclusion is biased and subjective. They would prefer that we get our second opinion from within the same medical group. We are insisting that we go outside our group and get that opinion from the City of Hope. Therefore, we are scheduled for an appointment August 16. We will pay for that exam and assessment out of pocket. Unfortunately, our care at City of Hope stops there unless we are successful in the appeal process with Blue Shield. Not an easy task, we are finding out.

Sue remains in good spirits and we would expect nothing less. We are also awaiting a visit from our daughter Suzanne and 3 of our grandchildren on August 15th. We want that visit to be upbeat and fun.

Working our way through the medical bureaucracy is a daunting task and a learning process.

Will keep you posted......As always, Bill

Date: Thursday, August 18, 2011 1:05 PM

Hi.....Well, I completed my first round of chemo treatment last Thursday, however, they had to do the second drug "of choice" on Friday, also. Next treatment will be Sept. 2, and hopefully they will be able to do the entire treatment in one day. On Thursday, I didn't have any side affects but after the lengthy treatment of Alimta on Friday, I was really wiped out until Tuesday morning. Thursday was Avastin and Cisplatin. I'm throwing all of this out to you all because I want you to be "impressed." Not sure why, but so be it. I couldn't keep my eyes open for more than a few hours at a time after the Alimta but come Tuesday morning I was feeling more like myself. We actually stayed at a motel Monday night before the City of Hope second opinion. The appt. was at 8 am and we didn't want to fight the traffic of working people trying to get to their jobs early Tuesday. That worked out pretty well, and I even had a good-sized breakfast before the City of Hope appt.

City of Hope went well as I met with one of the top rated Polish female doctors in the business. I put a lot of pressure on her to give me lots of tender love and care because I am, too, 100% Polish. That doesn't surprise many people, I know. She was somewhat encouraging in that she confirmed that the current scheduled treatment was right on the mark. She also confirmed that there might be some other drugs that may help me buy more time and better quality of life if I had the right DNA. I'm routing for the right DNA. We'll see more about that later in my treatments. We also met and talked with a number of other support staff at the City of Hope, that gave us the distinct impression that we would like to continue later on with my treatments there. Come December we will be able to switch to a PPO and Medicare supplement and will have more choices where I can get treated without all the current hassle we are dealing with. That's Bill's job handling all that advocate stuff. I couldn't have asked for or received a better husband, advocate and best friend than Bill is and always was.

Suzanne, Stephen, Eric and Kim arrived this past Monday, and we are keeping them very busy. Since the kids are bigger, does not make them easier to entertain. Bill has them at a marine biologist facility in La Jolla today taking in the sights and snorkeling. Kim is very interested in that field and has a cousin working here and will be showing her the ropes. Very exciting for them. I'm taking the day off to catch up on the wash, a little housekeeping and of course, line dancing this afternoon. Unfortunately, they won't let me get a pedicure or dye my hair because of the chemicals and germs, so I'll have to deal with that myself. At least I haven't lost any hair yet and maybe won't. Bill and I actually picked out a wig last week, and since I can't remain blonde for a while, maybe I'll pick up that wig after all.

So, all's pretty good right now, and since I kinda know what to expect for the future treatments, I'm more prepared to deal with the affects with a little less trepidation. How ironic, however, I've been trying to stay trim for the last 6 years and now that I have this, I actually need to be aware of keeping more weight on than off. Right now I'm 136 but would like to get back to about 140 before the next treatment. My mind says one thing and my stomach says another. All those classes I've taught in the past are well instilled in me about staying fit and trim, eating right, exercising because they will all help you live longer. What the hell happened?! Thanks for all your well wishes, heartfelt thoughts and prayers and keeping in touch. We have a very positive attitude and approach to this problem. Without all my family, friends and neighbors, not to miss classmates, this wouldn't be as tolerable as it is. So, we will keep on keeping on.......Love, Susie

Date: Friday, September 2, 2011 7:22 PM

I am emailing everyone today because for the next 3 days I will be somewhat comatose. Lots a sleep time to allow the chemo to work. I am more prepared this time around, as I cooked meals ahead in order to make Bill look good at "cooking"........that would be warming stuff up....but I won't burst his "cooking" bubble. I plan on plenty of sleep and not feeling a bit guilty about it. The actual chemo treatment was done all in one day and took just over 4 hours. I tried to do some reading but I was busy talking with a gentleman patient being treated for a different cancer. He was real talkative, then just when I was getting into the conversation, he had the nerve to fall asleep....and he was only about 50....go figure. I can still run circles around most and especially this guy. He even had the nerve to tell me that he and his wife had pedicures and manicures together. First of all, if I was the guy, I don't think I'd be bragging about a pedicure much less a manicure. What really ticked me off was that I didn't get my pedicure last week because I talked with the nurse and she said NO........I guess this guy acted first and then found out later. He's a better "man" than I "gungadin". You live and learn....

Some good news this past week. A new drug was approved by the FDA called Xalkori for patients with ALK Mutation (non-small cell lung cancer who are ALK positive). Not sure if I qualify as they have not done a biopsy yet. Talking about that.....at City of Hope, Dr. Marianna Koczywas, I love that name......anyways, she said she would have had the biopsy done right away. Well, I just had to mention that to my oncologist today and he also got her second opinion report, that a biopsy would be very easy due to the fact that where the "mass" not really, but where they could take some tissue would be very easy to obtain.....would be done asap. Now, he never mentioned that fact to me, I had to tell him.....sooooooooo what did he do next, by golly he wrote a referral to have a biopsy scheduled in the very near future. Wow, what a guy! Glad he's so on the ball.....Even if I don't have that specific mutation, Dr. Koczywas would still use the new drug, since I am a "never smoked patient", and thought that even without the mutation, some benefit could still be had with the new drug. Gosh, I wonder if my oncologist could figure that out. Maybe I better mention that fact to him also. He wouldn't want Dr. Koczywas get one up on him.

My daughter, Suzanne, talked with a Doctor/ Teacher at the college she works at, and that person said that, "if you had a choice of which type of lung blood cancer you would get, non-small cell is the preferred." Seems like that is the better for either controlling or at best, remission. I'll take either right now. In my era, and that includes most of you out there, smaller usually meant better, think DIAMONDS.....but seems in this and/or my case, bigger is better. Maybe the target is bigger so that chemo has more to shoot at and hopefully destroy.

Well I guess I better get back to the Red Sox Game on Extra Innings....I always buy that package yearly.....they are not doing very well right now against Texas. But we are still 1/2 game ahead of the dreaded Yankees. I can feel myself drifting a little, so I hope I haven't rambled too much, or not......I should be good in about 3 or 4 days.....sleep tight, oh I mean me......Susie

The following is an article Susie wrote for the October 2011 monthly news letter she normally writes for but, this time, instead of fitness and nutrition bits and tips, she decided to get a bit more personal to encourage others who may be facing serious illnesses also.

Fitness and Nutrition Bits and Tips
By Sue Winslow, Resident

The "Older you get, the Wiser"?, "Living and Learning", and the one I like best; "The Older I get, the Smarter my Father gets". We are all certainly getting older, but I'm not so sure how much wiser. At this stage of most of our lives, "living and learning", seems to fit the best. Granted, circumstances usually dictate changes. What we do with that new information is the problem.

In addition, there are 3 words that have been thrown around a lot lately; Proactive, Reactive, and Complacent. Before I go any further, let me give you the most recent definition of each word.

Proactive; serving to prepare for, intervene in or control an expected occurrence or situation, especially a negative or difficult one; anticipatory.

Reactive; done in response to a problem or situation; reacting to problems when they occur instead of doing something to prevent them.

Complacent; contented to a fault, self-satisfied and unconcerned, unaware of possible dangers, being pleased to a point of doing nothing, a feeling of acute contentment to the point of causing loss of one's self.

Wow, eye opening, right? Thought you knew what word best describes yourself. I sure was. Most of my life I have seen myself as Proactive, but I have to admit a lot of the time I was Reactive or even Complacent. The latter two sure are easier to do, especially when you are young and shall I say "less wiser". Living in a senior community, we don't have that luxury any longer. As we age, the chances of getting debilitating diseases or chronic illnesses is very high. Can we step out of our very familiar comfort zone into a bit of a discomfort zone and protect ourselves from the more than likely oncoming health problems.

The good thing this year, for the first time, everyone can get quality health care coverage even if you have a pre-existing health condition. That is a Christmas gift and/or Birthday gift all wrapped up in one. Since this opportunity has come our way, and that includes non-seniors as well as seniors, you owe it to yourself and family to really investigate your options. Don't do as we did and go the most affordable route and not anticipate a catastrophic illness that could strangle anyone's financial status. A year ago we decided to do just that. After all, neither of us had a family history of any catastrophic diseases and therefore "tried" a year of HMO coverage. Within 9 months, all hell broke loose. We had to scramble to find what options we had to help alleviate some of the financial stress. Fortunately, that happened to our benefit, but not without a lot of phone calls and paperwork.

Since the "new year" for health coverage begins this October 15 to December 15, we all have the good fortune of searching, calling and asking a lot of important questions. What is the best course of action to take to give your family the best chance at real quality health care without burdening your livelihood. Quality doesn't have just one meaning when it comes to health coverage. Having the right to make your best choices of doctors and health care facilities has been the biggest challenge. Don't "short change" those options. Take the time to read the small print. Don't hesitate to ask your friends or neighbors regarding their experiences in determining what health plans work for them. A lot can be learned.

Bottom line; you now have the Golden Opportunity to become PROACTIVE.

All in all, life is pretty darn good. It seems I have been given more time, and Bill and I are thankful for that. I am not one to waste time and don't intend to in the future. We will just keep on keeping on.

Age of enlightenment

I believe we are entering into an age of enlightenment (some would rather call it the end-times) in the very near future. All the signs of an economic collapse, increasing bad weather, and the many natural disasters are some indication that God is about to reveal Himself very soon. Those who are ready for this are becoming enlightened as time continues on.

Enlightenment in a secular context often means the "full comprehension of a situation," but in spiritual terms the word alludes to a spiritual revelation or deep insight into the meaning and purpose of all things, communication with or understanding of the mind of God, profound spiritual understanding or a fundamentally changed consciousness whereby everything is perceived as a unity.

Some scientists believe that during meditative states leading up to the subjective experience of enlightenment, there are actual physical changes in the brain. These changes are likely the beginning of what many feel happens when we enter the New Age of enlightenment or the "Age of Aquarius"

In **new age christianity**, enlightenment is obtained by direct infusion from the Sacred Rays. The Sacred Rays are continuous streams of energy, consciousness, love and data from the Godhead that is color coded into 12 different frequencies. This energy is above gamma rays and not observable by current science. Nevertheless, these Rays can supposedly be caught by the higher self's five different chakras, and then absorbed into the meditator's more physical bodies, and retained within the seven lower chakras, or the seven churches of John's Revelation. There are 12 human chakras in this system, total.

There are also 12 petals on the heart chakra in this system. Specifically, these 12 petals are also designed to catch and hold the 12 sacred energies of enlightenment. The theory goes that as the energy from the 12 Sacred Rays accumulates in the chakras and petals, the higher-self will eventually become activated.

This, in turn, allows the enlightened individual to displace and transcend the selfish ego and quickly develop supernatural abilities, including the fruits and the gifts of the Spirit, perfect peace, the realization of the unity of all things, raise kundalini, and develop the siddhas of Hinduism.

In this method, enlightenment is not accomplished by intellectual insight, dogmatic beliefs, or physical works. It is more a product of dedicated meditation, surrender to Spirit and absorption of God's grace, as contained in the Sacred Rays. This long process ultimately transforms "the old man" into "the new man." It is also considered to be the "New Birth" by New Age Christians.

It's going to happen, and I hope we are ready for it. You know if it is already happening by the thoughts and ideas that are coming to you. You think to yourself, am I giving up on all my old beliefs or am I just pipe dreaming?

Any way you cut it, God will and is a major part of what's happening. He is getting the world ready. Don't shut Him out. Let Him be a part of your plans and a part of your life, if He isn't already.

Chapter 8

We are living longer

than our ancestors

I wrote a lot of this book while rehabbing at a health care center after having a bone operation to prevent me from losing my right foot. I am diabetic and almost two years ago, after a minor bone scraping operation to heal a foot ulcer on the bottom of my foot, I contracted the staff infection MRSA. This is the infection all diabetics, and everyone else I suppose, are afraid to get. It is one of the hardest to combat because of its resistance to most antibiotics.

After believing we got it all out of my wounds, we found recently it had gotten into bone marrow of two little bones in my right foot. After an MRI was performed, my doctor said I have one of two choices; remove those infected bones and have a deformed foot with difficulty walking, or try a new procedure he felt could save my foot. Well, God bless this fine young surgeon for thinking outside the box. He did not do what most orthopaedic surgeons do, and cut off your foot in order to stop the spread of the infection. I opted for trying to save my foot. Eight weeks later, it looks like it worked, but he said he will feel better if the MRSA doesn't return during the next six months. So far, so good.

The reason I am telling you this story, while rehabbing in this care center, is that I have met many people over the age of 90 that are still going strong. One gentleman, Tony, was a fulltime fireman from NYC. He retired after 21 years in 1959, and has been receiving his retirement pension ever since. He is 97 years old (in 2011), and because I was a fulltime fireman for 7 years in upstate New York, we had a lot to talk about. He likes to play bingo, as many older folks do, and still laughs and enjoys life. There were many others like him, living longer than all expected they would many years ago.

Actuaries predicted that for Caucasian women in California, without arteriosclerosis (hardening of the arteries), the average life expectancy was 100. Now most life insurance companies say women outlive men and that may be true because there were at least four women over the age of 90 in the section where I was, and two men over the age of 90.

The major complaint I heard from most of them was, they wish they had taken better care of their health earlier in life. Knowing how long they are currently living, they wish they could enjoy their long life with better health. I am hoping if enough younger folks read this book, and try many of the suggestions given, these younger people won't have simular complaints while living longer.

What is driving us as we look towards the future?

Is it fear of disaster, an economic melt down, a desire to live healthier longer, or is it a spiritually inspired motivation to create a better world? For those of us who feel responsible for the condition of the world we live in, this is a burning question. If we are to work together to create the next steps, that so urgently need to be taken, it is essential that we begin to articulate and agree upon the values and principles that will guide us in reaching our goals.

Forming groups of like-minded individuals and agreeing on how and what we can do to save our ego system and other factors that are causing damage to this earth God gave us to care for is a step in the right direction. Now that we know we will be living longer, my main concern is, what will the environment be like

10 to20 years from now. I am 70, and I may still be around then. I know my children and grandchildren will be.

Making a better world to live in will make for an easier way to survive and stay healthy. This earth God gave us, as pictured in the Garden of Eden, can still become a reality if we strive to work together to make it so. This will give use that "Wee Bit Of Heaven."

What do you expect your second lifetime to be as you get older?
Can you envision a rising arc of expectations after you turn 50 (your second lifetime)? That's the challenge facing each of us, as well as society as a whole. The current turmoil over deficits and entitlements centers on taking care of the elderly, yet few realize how profound a shift has occurred. As stated, the life expectancy has risen every decade in modern times; now the Japanese lead the world with an overall life expectancy of 82.3 years, with the U.S. well down the list at 78.3 years. However, these figures are measured from birth. Your chances of living a very long time increase the older you get, so that a 70-year-old has a better chance of living to be 80 than a younger person.

To come to terms with our extending years, society has focused on two measures. One is economic. We have to figure out how to house and care for an aging population. The other is medical. In 2004 the elderly (65 years of age or older) amounted to 12 percent of the population, but 34 percent of health costs, about five times more than for children. This figure skews dramatically in the final years of life; about 25 percent of all the medical care a person pays for over a lifetime is laid out for their final illness, the one, ironically, that they will not survive. As everyone has heard by now, the disproportion of medical care for the aged is going to take off as baby boomers, now in their 60s, get even older.

Quality of life and spiritual growth

We no longer sit our aging population in rocking chairs and expect them to stay on the sidelines. The "new old age," which defines old age as a positive and active time of life, has been with us for at least two decades. Baby boomers, who are famous for wanting the best lifestyle at every age, extend this expectation far beyond earlier generations. When asked by pollsters to name the year that old age begins, the average answer from baby boomers was 85! If you read the obituaries, no doubt you have noticed that those who die between 65 and 75, which seemed normal a few decades ago, now seem to have been taken away at a shockingly young age.

If you can make it to 70 or older, you will (as long as your health allows) find that you are not ready for the rocking chair generation. To stay young, even though your age says it's time to give up, by the younger generation, don't listen. Let your desires and aspirations take you into your new future. The world still has a lot to offer and when life stands still, then life ends.

If your spiritual beliefs need re-evaluating, don't fear, as this may be God talking to you. Old folks often have the tendency to stay in a rut, and their minds begin to shut down when something new is presented. Don't let this happen. Let your mind be as sharp as it has ever been giving new ideas a fair consideration. The world is constantly changing, and new thoughts and old ways can often work together.

Looking at the big picture

I think the big picture is ultimately a spiritual question. Looking toward the horizon of old age, which is rapidly approaching for almost everyone I know, as well as for society as a whole. I wonder what spiritual changes are afoot. Although I covered a lot of what I believe earlier, I still wonder, as I am sure many of you do also, what the future holds..

Your attitude determines your future

Do you realize you are creating your future by the very attitude you posses?

Take a look at Proverbs 15:15. The Amplified Bible says it this way, "All the days of the desponding afflicted are made evil (by anxious thoughts and foreboding), but he who has a glad heart has a continual feast (regardless of circumstances)."

We have an "either - or" situation here. Have a glad heart and a continual feast, or have your days made evil by "stinking thinking." It's all an attitude.

Your attitude is supported by your beliefs, and your beliefs are vital to your success or failure in life. Jesus said, "As you have believed, let it be done unto you" (Matthew 8:13).

Whatever emotion you experience at any given time, is supported by a particular belief. If you are experiencing joy, there is an underlying belief that supports that emotion. If you are experiencing discouragement, there is an underlying belief supporting that too.

If you know God is taking care of you and watching out for your best interest, then relax. Have a glad heart and know He is in control, for the peace of God surpasses all understanding (Phil 4:7)

Do hard times determine your future?

.

Hard times do not always mean you have hit bottom financially. It also means you have given up on worldly things and will settle for the natural way of life. After leaving the world as we know it today, and entering into the basic way of living, you find yourself in an unknown phase of life.

Embracing your purpose in life is not limited to your comfort zone. The unknown is a place where you may be uncomfortable physically, spiritually or psychologically. Yet, this may be the place where your future is determined. Your purpose is tested and strengthened during these times. The unknown is a place where you have all your T's crossed and your I's dotted so that your great purpose can unfold.

Often we are convinced that we are forsaken and forgotten during this time. Sometimes we may only see a few steps ahead. By taking the few steps we can see, we discover the next steps that we do not see.

During this time of uncertainty, surround yourself with quality of people who come to your cause and not just those who come to your success! Don't be concerned about looking

successful, nor seeing yourself as a failure during your unknown journey. Allow others who
have made it through their own time of searching to come alongside you. Watch your purpose unfold in ways you never would have
known without your journey into the unknown.

Take courage, the hard times your ancestors
faced is much different than what you will face
as modern homesteaders seeking health, peace
with God, and a knowledge that if we need to
be a survivalist, we are able to succeed at it.

Conclusion

There is old saying, or some call a cliché, that says, "You can lead a horse to water, but you can't make it drink." This is the feeling I get as I write this book. Like most of the world, many have to have someone close to them die, without life insurance, before they realize the need to buy life insurance, or have a good savings account, for their family's protection.

This is what this book is all about. A life insurance in case of a disaster, and a savings account for when the time comes, and we all hope won't, when we need to survive on the "fruits of our own labor," another cliché.

As anyone who has a good monetary savings account will tell you, if you don't have to use your savings for emergency purposes, then you have the freedom of mind that everything will be alright when the time may come.

I hope as you have read the entire book, you realize that a disaster can happen anytime, anywhere. Furthermore, you have to be living somewhere without contact with any media to know the nation is heading into a financial melt down. We just don't know when.

Moreover, don't forget the health hazards we face everyday, handed to us by all the processing of the food we buy from the markets. Homesteading gives you the confidence to know what has gone into your food. Storing up the food you grow and raise gives you that savings bank account in your pantry and storage bins, and not insolvent banking institutions.

When God planned for our health and well-being, He gave us everything we needed to live a long and healthy life. The lifestyle we choose to live determines the conditions that will be facing us in the very near future.

As for my family, and me, we choose to live according to God's plan. And when we do, we will be exposed to "A Wee Bit Of Heaven."

Index

Symbols

"100-year flood" 22
100-year flood plane 23
1st Timothy 5:8 41
4-H project 123
5-gallon containers 114

A

A community of like believers 152
Active involvement in healing 176
Acts 2: 44-47 152
Age of Enlightenment 188
Almond 52
Aloe 53
American Heart Association 92
Amish people 153
Angora goats 80
Apple 54
Apples 101
arteriosclerosis 194
Attend Auctions 155
Attitude Determines Your Future 199

B

Barter System 162
barter system 160
bath canning, 106
Beans 54
beets 115
Behaviors 122
benefits of eating and raising rabbits 81

Big government 16
big picture 198
Bill & Susie 177
Black Beauty hens 118
Boer goat 79
bovine growth hormone (rbGH) 87
Boy Scout Motto 22
Breeding 132
Breeding Nigerian Dairy Goats 143
breeds of chickens 118
broomstick method 136
Buying Rabbits 131

C

cabbage 61
Cabrito 91
cancer prevention 48
cancer-protective B vitamin 88
Canning Fresh Fruits and Vegetables 103
Care 121
CB radios 159
Chevon 91
chicken tractor 76
Chickens 87
chickens 75
chickens inside city limits 116
Chicks need starter feed 119
climate change 21
compost 112
Connecting with others 153
Cons: 125
Container gardening 113
Container Plantings 146
Containers 113
Copper and Tin 163
Corn 55
Corn silk 55
Curing Vegetables to Improve Shelf-life 97

D

Daily meditation and prayer 170
Dehydrated 38
Dietary Supplement Labeling Act 44
Dill 56
Divine method 172
DNA technology 87
Dr. Carey A. Reams 49
Dual-purpose chickens 119
dwarf fruit trees 145

E

E. coli O157:H7 83
earth quakes in Japan 21
egg color 119
ego system 195
Emergency water and food supplies 36
Energy Efficient Steam Canner 106
Enlightenment 189
Ezekiel 47:12 52

F

Farmers Market 162
Feed 129
Feeding 140
Feeding/Watering 119
Fencing 139
fiat money 161
Figs 56
first aid supplies 32
first aid treatments 33
Fitness and Nutrition Bits and Tips 185
Food 68
Frasier Park 29
Freeze-dried 38
fruit trees 68

G

Garden of Eden 196
Gardening 71
Garlic 56
Gen. 1:29 51
Getting Started 127
giant breeds 131
gifts of the Spirit 190
Glenn Kimball 166
Go to the Library 154
Goat Milk vs. Cow Milk 93
Goats 91
goats 78
Gold and Silver 163
Grapes 56
Green onions 115

H

Handling of Specific Vegetables and Fruits 98
Hard Times 200
Healing herbs 51
Health 142
heat-resistant bacteria 105
heavy snow 29
High acid food 105
Hinduism 190
holistic in health care 50
holistic or homeopathic approach 51
homesteading 62
Honey 57
hormones 84
hormones used in food production 85
Housing 66, 127, 140
How Many Rabbits to Start? 130

I

Impending world collapse 19

Institute of Health Sciences 49
Irish Potatoes 98
Items to barter 161

J

Japanese 196
Jesus 172
John's Revelation 189

K

kundalini 190

L

Land 64
lemon juice 48
like-minded individuals 195
liquid fertilizer 73
Livestock 68
Living in smaller spaces 109
Local Home Schooling Groups 155
look towards the future 195
Luke 12:24 170

M

Mark 15:34 171
Mason bee hives 150
Mason Bees 147
Mathew 25:40 25
Matthew 10:29-30 170
Matthew 26:36-39 172
Matthew 8:13 199
Meat chickens 119
Medical Advisory 59
mini-garden 113
miniature goats 138
Mint 57
Multi-tree Plantings 146

N

nation of takers. 17
National Online Homestead Forum 156
natural catastrophe 27
Neighbour-hood Watch groups 158
New Age Christianity 189
new old age 197
New Zealand Whites 131
niacin 88
Nigerian Dwarf goat 79
Nigerian dwarf goats 139
Norman Cousins 176
North Dakota State University 82
Nutrients in Goat Meat 92
Nutrition 122

O

off the grid 27
off the grid. 63
Olive Oil 57
Onion 58
Onions 99
OTC vitamins and drugs 44
Other Equipment 129
Out-buildings 68

P

parasites, (worms, lice, fleas, ticks 142
Pears 102
Penny Saver magazine 162
Phil 4:7 199
Planting fruit trees 69
Plants that work well in containers 116
Poland 61
Pollinating your plants 147
pond 65
Preparedness and self-sufficiency 157

pressure canning 107
PROACTIVE 188
property tax 61
Pros: 124
Proverbs 15:15 199
Proverbs 16:24 169
Pumpkins 101

Q

Quality of life 197

R

Rabbit meat 81
Rabbits 89
radishes 115
Raising Chickens 117
Raising Rabbits 123
raising rabbits 81
Reuters 43
Robert Frost 165
Root crops 97
Russia 61
Rye 58

S

Sacred Rays 189
Science Of Spiritual Healing 173
second lifetime 196
Seeding and Transplanting 115
Sen. Durbin's dangerous Dietary Supplement Labelin 47
short-wave 159
size of garden 71
Slaughtering and Butchering 134
sludge 74
Social justice 18
Sodium hypochlorite 96
Soil and Fertilizers 114

soul 171
Soviet Union 20
Special Care 141
Specialized Pollinators 149
spiritual beliefs 198
spiritual growth 197
Square foot gardening 110
Standard & Poor's 43
Start an Online Yahoo Group 154
State and Local Governments 16
Stephen Moore 17
Storing your fresh fruits and vegetables 95
style of garden 71
survival 52
survive 166
Swap Meet 162
Sweet and Hot Peppers 99
symptoms of a stroke 35

T

Tax implications 160
Tetanus C and D shot 141
The demise of the United States 19
Thoreau 18
Tiered Plantings 147
To clean or not to clean before storage 96
Tomatoes 100
Trade Good Suppliers 162
Types of goat meat 91

U

Upstate New York 27
Utilities 67

V

vegetables 68
Vinegar 58

W

walkie-talkies 159
Wall Street Journal 17
Walnut 59
water-borne bacteria or fungi 96
Watering 115
white eggs 118
White Leghorn chickens 118
Winter Squash 101
without electricity 29
wood-burning stove 29

Y

Your Farmers' Supply or Feed Store 155
Your local 4-H group 154

Z

Zero Hedge 20